DELIBERATE INTERVENTION

Using Policy and Design to
Blunt the Harms of New Technology

by

ALEXANDRA SCHMIDT

foreword by Enrique Martinez

TWO WAVES
BOOKS

TWO WAVES BOOKS
NEW YORK, NY, USA

Testimonials

"*Deliberate Intervention* is an in-depth, thoroughly cited guide on the intersection of policy and design, employing a narrative style that makes the complex subject matter fun to read and easy to grok without losing any of its gravitas. An absolute must-read for any citizen designer."

—Lisa Baskett,
Healthcare Design Strategist

"What will it take to design technology that does less harm? This subtle book offers thoughtful, nuanced, sometimes unexpected answers. It's a good read for any curious user of technology. And for anyone who shapes or regulates new products, reading it is a step toward doing good by designing well."

—Conor Friedersdorf,
Staff Writer, *The Atlantic*

"This book is what America needs right now. With our democracy in dire straits and tech companies threatening our rights and privacy, the need for us to be proactive about policy is at an all-time high."

—Ginger Reinauer,
Senior Product Designer

"This book is an important resource for people in civic tech looking to navigate the complex relationship between policy, design, and technology. I wish it had existed earlier in my career!"

—Eddie Tejeda,
Civic Technologist and Engineering Director

"Alex provides a novel lens based on the intersection of design and policy. Her book provides an excellent foothold for creating beloved and successful products that minimize potential harms. It also helps policymakers more thoroughly consider their approach in the design of new regulation. It's essential reading for those who want to help their organization become more effective while making the world a better place."

—Theo Linnemann,
Computer Scientist and Technology Evangelist

Deliberate Intervention
Using Policy and Design to Blunt the Harms of New Technology
By Alexandra Schmidt

Rosenfeld Media, LLC
125 Maiden Lane
New York, New York 10038
USA

On the Web: www.rosenfeldmedia.com
Please send errata to: errata@rosenfeldmedia.com

Publisher: Louis Rosenfeld
Managing Editor: Marta Justak
Interior Layout: Danielle Foster
Cover Design: Heads of State
Illustrator: MJ Broadbent
Indexer: Marilyn Augst
Proofreader: Sue Boshers

ISBN: 1-933820-15-2
ISBN 13: 978-1-933820-15-6
LCCN: 2022942993

Printed and bound in the United States of America

Contents at a Glance

Contents and Executive Summary

Many—in the design world and outside of it—feel that something is not right with the development of our technology. This book is for those people to think more deeply about the intersection of design (which produces technology, typically in the private sector) and policy (which constrains and shapes new technology, typically from the public sector).

Humans are usually not great at predicting the future. And as technology develops at an ever more rapid pace, our responses to it are becoming all the more reactive.

While policy and design have similar processes, they have different underlying drivers. Rather than being contradictory, one could view them as complementary to each other.

From railroads to flammable clothing, evident harms are often the catalyst that lead to policy interventions. This chapter is a brief history of nondigital technologies, with digital technologies covered in later chapters.

With their complementary lenses in shaping the future, policy and design can move closer together to collaborate—and in fact, they are already doing so in notable ways.

Those who work in the public sector are using design methods to create better policy—another illustration of the idea that these spheres are moving closer together.

A sort of postscript, this chapter is a call to get excited about working on our complex, policy-constrained challenges.

The problem of "shaping" our new designs and technologies is a difficult one. Small, directional improvements may be the best approach we have.

Foreword

Logic would dictate that tech innovations can only add value to our lives; that, when they are widely adopted, it must be because they are good enough to be good forever.

Alex Schmidt explains how technology impacts the drivers of change at play in our society, such as public interest, democratic governance, or individual rights. She does it from a designer's perspective, which is always a tug of war between opposites: me/we, present/future, benefit/harm, etc.

Take one of those opposites: intended benefit versus unintended harm. I used to bring to class a big, sharp, kitchen knife when I wanted to discuss its use and misuse with my industrial design students. I asked them to gather in a circle, shoulder to shoulder, and hold the knife for a few minutes, in turn. In the kitchen, we use the knife as it was designed to be used, but an unexpected new context quickly sends the knife holder on a thinking spiral that reveals the object's dark side: it can also be misused to harm others.

Deliberate Intervention brings you to a place of reckoning that questions how technology adds value to our volatile society. It is an invitation to reflect on how social context, culture, and variable time horizons transform the world and how those transformations, activated by technology, can drift to dark places. If you believe that, even if we can't predict the future, at least we can design it, this book may change your mind.

Alex's understanding of design at the deep level of its social implications supports the claim that what we may design today with the best of intentions will likely evolve into something quite different tomorrow. Savor that thought—one of the golden nuggets of this book—if you agree that, although imperfect, the practice of design is still the best chance we have to add value to the lives of many.

This book is a journey at different altitudes that invites you to reflect on what you read from your own personal experience: is design really compatible with policymaking? Is harm the side effect of large-scale structural change? Is it ethical to stick to a laissez-faire approach to the urgent challenges we are facing?

Tick tock, tick tock…

Whether you decide to fly high or wander close to the ground, *Deliberate Intervention* will help you come up with new questions; that's what it was designed for.

—Enrique Martínez,
Designer and Strategic Innovation Adviser

Introduction
Something's Not Right

Some years back, I was working at a small design and software agency when I got interested in the topic of privacy. Despite my work in the tech space, I have always been a bit of a tech doubter, if not a full-on technophobe. As I saw it, tech behemoths were hollowing out some of the things I cared most about, like small businesses that create sustainable jobs and make communities vibrant, local journalism which sits at the heart of democracy, and even the concept of truth itself. At the time, "privacy" seemed like a way for me to try to understand and describe problems of new technology, along with my role as a design person within them. Since I have a background in journalism, I did what felt familiar: interviewed a bunch of people and wrote articles about privacy, informed consent, and other ideas in the privacy and design space.

Since that time, I have noticed that other design folks sometimes follow a similar path—they feel like something is "not right," and they focus on privacy as "a way in" to understanding what it is and their role in it. Lately, the "something is not right" and "how do I understand" has evolved beyond privacy. It now includes new topics, such as bias in algorithms and AI (particularly facial recognition). Concerns with tech ethics, humane design, and systems design are all, I would argue, ways of trying to make sense of the feeling that "something is not right."

I decided to pick a policy lens because it felt encompassing and durable. While different tech boogeymen—privacy, drones, deep fakes—may come and go, they will hopefully always be informed and shaped by policy at a wider societal level. Likewise, policy itself is shaped by design as it emerges. I hope that this lens will endure and provide a helpful way for thinking through both current and future issues around tech harms.

Design Can't Save the World

As noted, many in the design community have responded to the feeling that something is not right by calling for more ethics in design. There are countless ethical toolkits, trainings, and frameworks available for design professionals to become more thoughtful in their work. Designers can take a pledge to adopt a code of ethics, and there have even been calls for professional licensing that includes a sort of Hippocratic oath for design.

These efforts are laudable when one considers that the drive for profit in private companies can end up overshadowing ethical considerations. But this book centers on the notion that placing the responsibility on individual designers to fix these problems through "ethics" is insufficient as a single response, particularly when capitalism is the paradigm they function in. Beyond those individuals, reducing the harms of digital technology is simply too big a challenge for the private sector to address on its own. Thus, the policy sphere—motivated (ideally) by values over profit—has a key role to play. In other words, designers alone can't save the world. But, thankfully, the challenges at hand do not rest solely on their shoulders.

Overarching Concepts of This Book

I do not consider myself a subject matter expert in the areas covered in this book. Rather, I see my value-add as the research and "pulling together" of the wisdom and experiences of others. Nearly every concept in this book has a whole universe of writing, thought, and scholarship behind it. So, I have struggled to find a balance between standing on the shoulders of giants, while also presenting certain ideas and concepts as my own.

As the journalist Adrian Nicole LeBlanc has said, "Once I've written about something, I'm ready to write about it." Coming up with a basic overarching structure for this book was a torturous experience that involved many twists and turns. Only in the process of writing did I really come to understand what it was about. I am grateful to Marta Justak and Lou Rosenfeld for bearing with my (unusual for Rosenfeld Media) journalistic approach to writing this book.

On the arc of the book, once it all came together, it felt quite logical in my mind. But I want to make sure that clarity comes through strongly to readers as well. So, we've decided to make the arc visible with a chapter map, illustrated by the incomparable MJ Broadbent.

Big picture, the book is roughly structured around how harms emerge from designs, and how policy comes to constrain those harms. But we'll look at those key concepts from a number of different angles—what it's like to design in "unconstrained" spaces vis-à-vis "constrained" spaces, how to bring policy and design closer together, and how to tackle enterprise design challenges. These different concepts sometimes connect to each other, even if they are not next door to each other in the book's chronology. With these varied slices and dimensions, and a chapter map to guide, a broad mental model for the space should be presented.

NOTE ➤ **Geographic Perspective**

This book is written with a focus on the U.S. with key exceptions in a few places. While digital technology and certainly the internet are global, writing a book that encompasses all policy approaches in the world would not have been possible. I also believe that, while different countries have different systems of government and regulations, many of the basic patterns identified here around how new technology and policy emerge will hold true from country to country.

Who Is "We"?

In this book, I often use the frame of "we," so it's important to acknowledge who I imagine that to be. I see an audience in people involved in designing and building technology, people working on tech policy, and anyone looking at technology design and wondering, "What is wrong?" While certain aspects of the book may be a bit "designer insider baseball," there are broader ideas here that extend far beyond the field of design.

This Book's Biases

I am keenly aware of how the randomness and individuality of my experiences informs my point of view, and it's important for me to reveal my biases. As already mentioned, I am, by nature, a bit of a technophobe. I believe this is connected to a critical nature—a desire to question and not accept everything that comes my way. In addition to this slightly rebellious spirit, I find that thinking about things critically is fun, so much so that I have a Master's degree in Cultural Reporting and Criticism.

I believe government has the capacity to be a force for good in people's lives, while acknowledging that it has often failed to live up to that potential. Government's use of autonomous weapons, and the desire to be unshackled by any constraints around their use, is a dismal example. The disproportionate harms perpetrated on Black Americans, Native Americans, and others, both historically and still today, is likewise dispiriting.

Still, to me, at its most ideal, government is simply everyone deciding to work together to solve collective problems, and it is incidental that "government" is the vehicle by which we do so. I find a lot of hope in that concept and believe there is promise in it. I also believe that, when reasonably constrained, capitalism can be a force for good in the world as well. I am not an "either/or" thinker when it comes to government and capitalism. Rather, I am optimistic that the public and private sectors working more closely together can be a powerful engine for problem solving. This book takes as a given that, while neither is perfect, they are what we have, and are likely to have, for a while.

I have tried to reach beyond the biases and privilege baked into my upbringing (upper middle class, Jewish, heterosexual, cisgender, American born). My father set a strong example of volunteerism, traveling as a doctor to his home country of Mexico, as well as Ethiopia and Haiti on medical missions to help people different from him. I hope I have captured that spirit in trying to reach out to people with diverse backgrounds, experiences, and perspectives to inform this book. My points of view have been impacted and altered by this research, and I am grateful to those who have taken the time—either person-to-person or through their writing—to educate me. I am sure I still have blind spots and welcome critiques that point out what I have missed.

An Evolving Story

While this book is optimistic, it is also, I hope, not naive. I wrote it in 2021 during a window of time when the forces of liberal democracy seemed to be on a (perhaps brief) upswing in the United States. But there is no doubt that those fundamentals are and have been at risk for some time. The influence of money in U.S. politics makes leaders much less beholden to the public, structures of aspects of our political system such as the Senate and Electoral College are not democratically representative, and forces sowing broad distrust in institutions have been on the rise for many decades as of this writing. As illiberalism and autocracy rise, and democratic institutions and public trust in them devolve—trends we see in places like Poland, India, Turkey, Brazil, and Hungary as well—the possibility that this book's ideas can be achieved (essentially, that government has a role to play in the design of new technologies) diminishes.

There is also the not inconsequential fact of the raw power of big tech, vis-à-vis nation states. In some cases, society has become so dependent on big tech that governments simply may not have the capacity to be the countervailing force I hope them to be. In one notable example, when Spain attempted to tax Google News in 2014 in order to distribute some of the aggregator's profits to news publishers whose content they used, the service withdrew from the country, and Spain backed down.

Still, I've decided to take a hopeful stance on the role of democratic government in shaping the world in recognition that we do not know what the future holds. There are examples of countries that have perhaps been through worse and come out on the other side. Nelson Mandela, the first democratically elected president of South Africa who led the country out of apartheid, and Václav Havel, the first democratically elected president of the Czech Republic after the fall of communism, are two examples that I often ponder. If the U.S. and other countries succumb to waves of autocracy presently on the rise, and democracy here takes a further downturn, there may well come a time when that reality shifts yet again.

Some of the most pressing issues at the bleeding edge of the policy and design space while this book was being written were bans of public officials from social media networks and facial recognition AI. Obviously, new technologies and debates will emerge, no doubt making these particular topics feel outdated. However, by taking a historical view of how new designs and technologies tend to emerge, this book should hopefully remain relevant, even as the landscape changes.

Something IS NOT RIGHT...

Proactive POLICY Reactive
It's hard to predict the future

BASICS
POLICY & DESIGN

HISTORIC EMERGENT HARMS
(NON-DIGITAL)

Present day EMERGENT HARMS
(DIGITAL)

INTERVENTIONS
Organizations create their own policy

EXTERNAL
INTERVENTIONS
Government policy in the digital sphere

Designing WITHIN
POLICY CONSTRAINTS

Bringing
POLICY & DESIGN
Closer Together

Bringing
DESIGN METHODS TO
POLICY CREATION

Enterprise Design and POLICY

WICKED PROBLEMS
and Baby Steps

1

A View of the Future

A father in a suburban U.S. town returns home after dropping his children off at school and unfastens his seatbelt, just in time to receive a package delivered by a drone. He walks inside and checks his retirement account on his phone, using facial recognition to log in. In a large city a few hundred miles away, an undocumented immigrant walks into his job at a restaurant. He has his movements tracked through his smartphone, unbeknownst to him, so that the spread of a new viral infection can be traced by health experts. Overseas, a deployed member of the military checks her social media feed and sees political ads regarding an upcoming election. She puts her phone in her pocket and walks to a nearby barracks for training on a new piece of military targeting technology.

Invisibly, these individuals are experiencing a designed world of technologies, tools, and built environment. Policies have in some cases brought these tools into being—think of government-funded GPS and the internet. And then, once the private sector promotes uptake among the public, policies constrain and shape those designs to varying degrees. In some cases—like a seatbelt in a car—policies that inform the design are well formed. In others, like the online bank account and health tracking, they are just beginning to emerge and take shape. And in yet others, like AI used in military technologies, few policies exist at all. As a result, the impacts of these technologies are felt in both predictable *and* unpredictable ways. Society is shaped by the technologies as they emerge, and in turn, society responds and shapes them back.

The act of forming policy to drive outcomes "in the public interest" (which we'll talk more about in Chapter 2, "Policy and Design Basics") has never been a simple undertaking. Both policy and design work on shaping the future, and they do so in varied, overlapping, and sometimes unpredictable ways. This book doesn't propose an elegant solution that will help the future come into being in a neatly planned-out fashion, which causes no harm to anyone. Rather, it offers a way for people working at the intersection of policy and design of new technology to think more clearly about these issues and understand their place in the puzzle better.

Increasing Speed and the "Pacing Problem"

Many thinkers and writers have detailed the increasing speed of technological progress. In the 1940s, economist Joseph Schumpeter wrote about the concept of "creative destruction," which he posited underpinned all societal progress. Creative destruction is the process by which existing business models are disrupted by newcomers, which Schumpeter called "the essential fact about capitalism."[1]

---

1. Joseph Schumpeter, *Capitalism, Socialism, and Democracy* (New York: Harper & Bros., 1942).

Such business growth has an extra fast, exponential flavor in the digital age, as Douglas Rushkoff observed in his book *Throwing Rocks at the Google Bus: How Growth Became the Enemy of Prosperity*. Venture capitalists buy companies not to own them, but to sell them at a steep profit. Because of that, there is a need by VC-backed companies to show quick disruption and exponential growth, rather than to build a slow and steady, sustainable company with a reliable customer base. That's why thriving companies like Twitter, which produced over $1 billion in revenue in 2020, are considered a failure—they produce revenue rather than growth. "A more realistically financed company gets to grow whenever it's appropriate," Rushkoff stated. "You get to grow at the rate of increasing demand rather than the rate demanded by your debt structure."

The speed of tech development is exacerbated by the development of technology itself. Gordon Moore, in what came to be known as Moore's Law, theorized when describing the development of semiconductors that the computing world would dramatically increase in power and decrease at a relative cost, at an exponential pace. Building on that insight came writers like Ray Kurzweil and his "Law of Accelerating Returns," which extrapolated Moore's insight from computing power more widely to all technology. R. Buckminster Fuller, an American architect, designer, and philosopher, theorized in his book *Critical Path* that human knowledge was increasing at an exponential rate—it doubled every 100 years in 1900, he theorized, then doubled every 25 years by the end of World War II, and so on.

Pull it all together, and we have a tech world evolving at a rapid pace. This trend has led to what's known as the "pacing problem," where technology moves ever faster, but policymakers move at the same speed as they always have. Regulatory agencies typically collect facts over a long period of time and engage in trial-like processes that go through multiple levels of oversight before being codified. When the U.S. Department of Justice sought to break up Microsoft in the late 1990s, for example, the case dragged on into the 2000s. By then, competitors like Google Chrome and Mozilla Firefox had appeared, rendering the case all but moot. Our current model of top-down enforcement, thoughtful as it is, may not be ideal for the rapidly moving technological environment we find ourselves in.

> *A run-of-the-mill UX'er is thinking 6 months out. Product innovation teams are looking 2-3 years out, standards people are 5 years out, deep academic research is 10 years out, and policy probably looks 15 years out.*
>
> —WHITNEY QUESENBERY,
> DIRECTOR AND CO-FOUNDER OF THE CENTER FOR CIVIC DESIGN

Proactive and Reactive Policy

A key concept to start out with is proactive and reactive policy, which we will revisit over the course of this book. Proactive policy shapes the future *ex ante*, before it has transpired. A current example of this involves the bans on the use of facial recognition software, with the IRS pulling back on a facial recognition scheme for tax filing before it had been tried. Reactive policy is *post hoc*, in response to something that has already occurred. An example of this could be safety requirements for refrigerators, which were implemented in 1956 in response to children getting caught in the appliances! As we'll see, most policy responses throughout history are reactive in nature. Indeed, facial recognition is widely used in the private sector, with proactive bans being far rarer.

The province of new designs is, typically and appropriately, that of the private sector. With their expertise in understanding customers and building things people want, marketing them and getting them used, it makes sense that private companies would work on creating "the new." Entrepreneurs and private companies do not typically ask for permission in creating what they do (though there come points in the development of any company when laws come into play, some of which may even halt progress). And herein lies the messiness—stuff gets built out there in the world and, if and when something goes wrong, policy-makers step in to "intervene."

At this point, we must ask: "Who gets to decide which interventions are appropriate and when they should be attempted?" Consider the Winston Churchill saying: "Democracy is the worst form of government, except for every other one." The idea is that, even if policies are not perfect, if they are implemented by leaders whom people have elected democratically to foster shared values and serve their interests, policies will be about as good as they can get. (Of course, whether particular democracies, including the U.S., are healthy and well-functioning is up for debate.)

Every new thing brings with it indisputable problems. "When you invent the ship, you also invent the shipwreck; when you invent the plane, you also invent the plane crash; and when you invent electricity, you invent electrocution," according to cultural theorist Paul Virilio.[2] There is no objective right or wrong about whether a new thing is or was good or bad, the thinking goes. Likewise, in some cases (particularly in the digital world), there is not always a clear answer as to what constitutes a "harm" of new technology, or what the right intervention should be to address it. Instead of coming up with the "right" answer, if we decide on these things together through transparent debate and a democratic system, we are more likely to achieve an outcome that the majority of us are happy with.

The Inscrutability of the Future and *Reactive* Policy

One of this book's arguments is that we typically cannot know the impacts of new designs or technologies until those things have had some time "out there," among people in the world, to make themselves

2. Paul Virilio, *Politics of the Very Worst* (New York: Semiotext(e), 1999).

known. History is littered with examples of worry about new things that later came to be assimilated and accepted as normal. For example, there was the fear that television and radio would lead to dangerous addiction, that photographs would lead to people collecting "fake friends," and that roller-skating could lead to charges of impropriety. See this excerpt from *The Chicago Tribune* of 1885, defending the roller skate against charges of impropriety (see Figure 1.1).

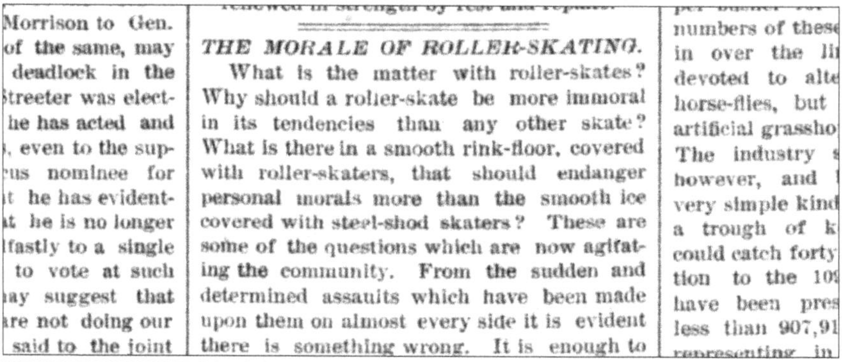

TWITTER ACCOUNT PESSIMISTS ARCHIVE @PESSIMISTSARC

FIGURE 1.1 A newspaper clipping expressing fear of the roller skate's negative side effects.

Writer Douglas Adams nicely sums up the worry about new things: "I've come up with a set of rules that describe our reactions to technologies:

"**1.** Anything that is in the world when you're born is normal and ordinary and is just a natural part of the way the world works.

"**2.** Anything that's invented between when you're fifteen and thirty-five is new and exciting and revolutionary and you can probably get a career in it.

"**3.** Anything invented after you're thirty-five is against the natural order of things."

Adams' theory doesn't mean that new technologies can't have negative side effects—they can, and they do. Think of the misidentification of Black people by facial recognition software leading to false arrests, or the countless deaths as a result of automobiles. But the point is that, from our subjective individual perspectives, we can't know which technologies will have mass uptake by the public, we can't usually know for sure what their negative effects will be ahead of time, and we often can't predict what the right policy interventions might be. There are too many unknown links in the chain of future events. This view means that policy tends to be "reactive" to the harms that we see emerging from technology.

> *The unimaginable is ordinary, [and] the way forward is almost never a straight line you can glance down but a convoluted path of surprises, gifts, and affliction you prepare for by accepting your blind spots as well as your intuitions.*
>
> —REBECCA SOLNIT,
> *HOPE IN THE DARK*

Notably, as policy attempts to shape the world, like design, it too produces unintended consequences. An example of an unintended consequence of well-meaning policy is cookie pop-ups (those notifications on websites asking you to "accept cookies") brought forth by EU regulations including the ePrivacy Directive and GDPR (General Data Protection Regulation). Because giving users control over their data has long been seen as the most ethical way of protecting privacy, it logically followed that every website should inform users of how their data would be used and seek their consent. Some years on, the pop-ups are widely panned as ruining the experience of the internet (see Figure 1.2). Future privacy legislation may seek to ban mass data collection outright, rather than put the onus on users for giving "consent"—thus removing the need for a pop-up at all. Just like design, policy is iterative as understanding evolves and unintended consequences make themselves known.

Andy Budd
@andybudd

···

A typical website visit in 2022

1. Figure out how to decline all but essential cookies
2. Close the support widget asking if I need help
3. Stop the auto-playing video
4. Close the "subscribe to our newsletter" pop-up
5. Try and remember why I came here in the first place

8:35 AM · Jan 2, 2022 · Twitter Web App

8,384 Retweets   **847** Quote Tweets   **39.9K** Likes

FIGURE 1.2 Cookie pop-ups have received broad criticism for "ruining" the experience of the internet, although they were intended to help protect user privacy.

DISPROPORTIONATE HARMS AND THINGS WE CAN PREDICT

Because we live in a world of racial, gendered, physical, and other hierarchies, our designs and technologies tend to reproduce inequities found in other parts of society. Thus, we can properly predict that every new technology will impact groups of people differently based on their place in this hierarchy. Just a couple of examples include the infrared soap dispenser that doesn't recognize dark skin, or public transit systems designed without elevators. In this light, it perhaps should not have been surprising that Twitter became a hotbed of abuse for women and other minorities. As Margaret Atwood wrote in *The Handmaid's Tale,* "Better never means better for everyone…It always means worse, for some."

CONTINUES ➤

CONTINUED ➤

Some thinkers in the design world thus caution against adopting a "universalist" lens for design and presuming to design for "everyone." As Sasha Costanza-Chock put it in their book, *Design Justice*, "Much, or perhaps most, design work imagines itself to be universal: designers intend to create objects, places, or systems that can be used by anybody. Design justice challenges the underlying assumption that it is possible to design for all people. Instead, we must always recognize the specificity of which kinds of users will benefit most." We'll explore ideas around proactive interventions to mitigate bias throughout the book and notably in Chapter 5, "Internal Interventions."

Making *Reactive* Policy as *Proactive* as Possible

The future's inscrutability does not mean we can't be a bit wiser about it as it starts to come into focus—about bias and other harms. By bringing policy and design closer together, society can attempt to shape technology more thoughtfully, rather than (just) the other way around. While we often can't know the impacts of technology until it's had some time in the world, we can make *reactive* responses as *proactive* as possible. This book will run through proactive and reactive responses to harms of tech, both in the private and public sectors, as well as provide some ideas for how these can move closer together.

The funny thing is that the tech world is very much fixated on the future and attempts to "hack" it—it's just that they're not trying to hack harms, but rather hack product-market fit and figure out which products will have uptake by users. VC firms run hundreds of "anthropological tech" experiments at a time to see which few ideas might stick, as a way to hack the inscrutable future and make it move faster.

And well they should focus on product-market fit. Without something that lots of people can *use*, we wouldn't be having this conversation about policy interventions to begin with. And there's the rub at the core of progress: We don't want to thwart innovation and progress, but as a society we need to also understand the trade-offs, and if and how to intervene. Makes you wonder what might happen if these firms ran similar experiments to anticipate future harms. Could we perceive them faster?

> *If we learn from revenge effects [or unintended consequences of technology], we will not be led to renounce technology, but we will instead refine it: watching for unforeseen problems, managing what we know are limited strengths, applying no less but also no more than is really needed...I am not arguing against change, but for a modest, tentative, and skeptical acceptance of it.*
>
> —EDWARD TENNER,
> *WHY THINGS BITE BACK: TECHNOLOGY AND THE REVENGE OF UNINTENDED CONSEQUENCES*

PULLING IT TOGETHER

The world we live in is invisibly shaped by designs we interact with and policies that go on to shape those designs. But in many spaces, humans are not good at predicting the impact of the new. On top of that, the speed at which new technologies enter society is increasing at a rapid pace. Thus, with some notable exceptions, policy tends to be more reactive than proactive in nature. By being a bit more thoughtful and collaborative, we can hope to be as proactive about our reactions as possible, and address harms as they emerge.

Something IS NOT RIGHT...

Proactive **POLICY** Reactive

It's hard to predict the future

BASICS POLICY & DESIGN

HISTORIC EMERGENT HARMS

(NON-DIGITAL)

Present day EMERGENT HARMS

(DIGITAL)

INTERVENTIONS

Organizations create their own policy

EXTERNAL INTERVENTIONS

Government policy in the digital sphere

Designing WITHIN POLICY CONSTRAINTS

Bringing POLICY & DESIGN

Closer Together

Bringing DESIGN METHODS TO POLICY CREATION

Enterprise Design and POLICY

WICKED PROBLEMS and **Baby Steps**

2

Policy and Design Basics

Conjure up a visual of Moses standing on a mountaintop with tablets in hand, and you can begin to understand the criticality of rules to our world. That event was so momentous that the Jewish people even have a holiday that exists purely to celebrate the receipt of law. Why so much excitement over edicts about what you can and cannot do? One need not think too hard to understand: if everyone operates by the same set of agreed-upon rules, conflicts can be adjudicated without violence. Society can run more smoothly, and we may hope to avoid the chaos of a Sopranos-like, mob-ruled world. A cause for celebration, indeed.

A cousin of law, "policy" is a usefully broad term that encompasses rules, guidelines, laws, and regulations. Michael Walton, senior lecturer in public policy at Harvard Kennedy School, defines policy as "an array of actions by collective actors designed to create or sustain a world in which we want to live." Those collective actors constitute:

- **Markets:** Companies that run as profit-making entities
- **Government:** The public sector
- **Civil Society:** Other groups of people, from small community organizations to religious groups to nonprofits

Notably, policy is not something generated only by government. Policy can be created or implemented by any of the policy actors outlined previously, whether that be a refund policy for goods sold in a store (markets), shaming others for not wearing masks during a pandemic (civil society), or, of course, government policy, such as emission standards for cars. This book will focus on policies as they arise in all of these spaces, with a particular focus on government policy.

"Design" is a term used broadly here to refer to a range of processes behind creation—whether the thing being created is software, services and physical products, or policy itself. Often, the things being designed in this book amount to new technologies, and the terms "design" and "technology" usually appear together.

Design can be practiced by people with the title "designer," or anyone else engaging in creative processes to generate something new. Because creating something new often entails making use of new or new-ish technology, the designer in question may be an engineer or software developer. Since so much of the output in need of policy today is in the software space, much of this book will be relevant for UX/UI designers, software developers, product managers, other people in technical spaces, or policymakers seeking to address those spaces. The experiences of these workers should serve as archetypes for those addressing new technologies, products, or processes as they come to be.

A NOTE ON "CIVIL SOCIETY"

While this book centers chiefly on the interplay of "markets" and "government," an astute reader might note the absence of "civil society" in this analysis of forces that shape the world. In fact, people acting "out there" in the world are often at the forefront of pushing government to act. As author and futurist John Naisbitt has quipped, leadership is the ability to "find a parade and get in front of it."

This book is not explicitly about civil society's role in shaping the world, but there are moments throughout where it is implied—nonprofits and other groups banding together to write guidelines for developing tech can be seen as civil society, as can anyone influencing government to act from "outside," of which there are many examples in Chapter 3, "A Brief History of Policy and New Technology." For the purposes of this book it's worth simply noting that activists in civil society have had real impact on policy and the design of our world, and will no doubt continue to do so.

> *[The history of disability advocacy] teaches us that it is indeed possible for a social movement to impact design policy, processes, practices, and outcomes in ways that are very broad, deep and long lasting. Disability rights and disability justice activists have changed federal policy, forced the adoption of new requirements in a wide range of design processes, altered the way many designers practice their craft, and significantly changed the quality of life for billions of people...*
>
> —SASHA COSTANZA-CHOCK,
> *DESIGN JUSTICE*

Policy and Design: Similar Processes, Differing Drivers

Both designers and policymakers work on creating and shaping the future. As such, practitioners in both spaces often speak of problems and solutions—they each have a practice of researching deeply and basing proposed solutions on a deeper understanding of the problem. Both spaces are iterative in nature, with prototypes and pilots in attempts to learn and see whether an intervention truly has value (see Figures 2.1a and b).

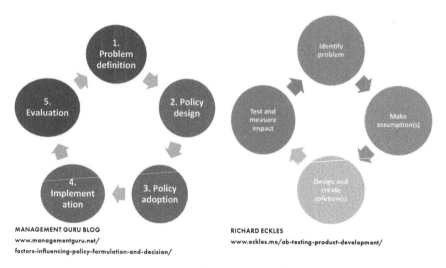

MANAGEMENT GURU BLOG
www.managementguru.net/
factors-influencing-policy-formulation-and-decision/

RICHARD ECKLES
www.eckles.me/ab-testing-product-development/

FIGURES 2.1A AND 2.1B Look similar? Here, the policy development cycle is on the left, and the product development cycle is on the right. Note, there are many varieties and flavors to both of these processes. The above diagrams are illustrative of overarching similarities.

Despite their twin purposes in creating the future, design and policy have very different drivers. From day one of their careers, UXers and other designers in the private sector are exhorted to focus on the user, remove pain points, provide delight, and in some cases "not make the user think," with the end goal being to generate profit within capitalism.

Meanwhile, government policymakers are, ideally (though not always in reality), driven by values and a desire to create public benefit. Such values and public benefits differ based on world geography and cultural background. Here, the concept of values-based viewpoints, or "normative frames," becomes useful. A normative frame in Western liberal democracies is that for all citizens, liberty is given equal weight. Ubuntu, a philosophy found in many African countries, defines humanity in relation to other people, or the individual in relation to the community.

> *Demonstrate ROI. In this approach, you gather and analyze data to prove that a usability change you've made resulted in cost savings or additional revenue.*
>
> —STEVE KRUG,
> *DON'T MAKE ME THINK: A COMMON SENSE APPROACH TO WEB USABILITY*

> *What kind of society do we want to live in? Every individual is likely to answer this question differently… The way in which we choose to use the tools of public policy to shape our communities always links back to our view of the societies in which we want to live.*
>
> —MICHAEL WALTON,
> SENIOR LECTURER, HARVARD KENNEDY SCHOOL

Neither the UX drive to focus on the user, nor policy's drive to focus on values, is better than the other. Each comes with its own strengths, weaknesses, and blind spots. For example, policy is often created in a vacuum, without understanding how actual people will experience or interact with it. Design practices could be valuable for improving people's experience of policy interventions. Meanwhile, UX's granular focus on the user can miss the implications of its work at the societal level. How might one bring "the erosion of democracy," caused by the proliferation of disinformation on social media networks, down to the level of the individual user experiencing those networks? Here, a policy lens could be useful to design. We will discuss these interplays much more in the coming chapters.

Where Does Government Policy "Take Place?"

While Chapter 6, "The Beginning of Outside Regulation," contains more detail on this, it's helpful to understand up front what is meant specifically by government policy, or the precise methods that government uses to shape the world we live in. In the strictest terms, governmental policy encompasses laws and regulations. Laws go through a bill process before becoming codified, moving (in the U.S.) from the House of Representatives to the Senate. Meanwhile, regulation is created by a governmental agency under the executive branch of government, and it does not go through this bill process. Regulatory agencies often hold public hearings on whether to adopt particular regulations.

Both laws and regulations may exist at multiple levels of government, from the local city level, up to state and federal levels. For example, in 2022, federal laws restricted the use of marijuana, while several states had laws on the books permitting it. In terms of regulation, the EPA currently issues federal emission standards for carmakers, while state environmental agencies might require their own detailed inspection of cars and trucks on a periodic basis.

Implementation of laws and regulations is where the rubber meets the road when it comes to shaping society. Depending on the law or regulation in question, implementation may include a number of things: the allocation of funds, awarding of incentives, or penalizing those who run afoul of rules. While many thoughtful laws and regulations may be passed, they sometimes fail when implementation is impractical or lacks follow-through.

Value Tension

While government policy is underpinned by values, it would be naive to believe that this renders policymaking a neat and simple process—pick your values and go from there (see Figure 2.2). Values are not in and of themselves "good." Consider the "value" of racial segregation, which led to separate drinking fountains during the Jim Crow era. Also, values sometimes conflict with one another, and can fluctuate in importance over time, depending on historic and political circumstances. Still, in an ideal world, public policy has the potential to be driven by a value system that is separate from the profit motive. This can serve as a counterbalance to the capitalism that drives many aspects of society.

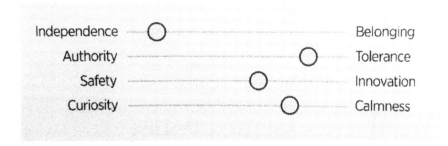

FIGURE 2.2 The "value spectrum," as proposed by Cennydd Bowles in his book *Future Ethics*, gauges where a given solution lies on various value spectrums.

The "public interest" is a concept that resonates strongly with notions of value in this book. Serving the public interest emerged as one of the key goals for regulating radio and railroads in the early part of the 20th century. What exactly constitutes "the public interest" has been hotly debated over the intervening years, in court cases and legislatures. Does the public interest reflect issues of access, social justice, or pocketbook issues? While some people posit that it cannot be pinned down as a concept and is always subjective, others believe it has value simply as something for government to "strive toward"—an ideal world in which public institutions serve the public.

The public interest standard can only be defined by the political culture of the historical moment in which that interpretation developed. As larger political and cultural changes impact how citizens, broadcasters, and regulators view broadcasting as a public forum, new identifiable definitions for the standard will continue to emerge.

—CHRISTINA LEFEVRE-GONZALEZ,
"RESTORING HISTORICAL UNDERSTANDINGS OF THE 'PUBLIC INTEREST'
STANDARD OF AMERICAN BROADCASTING: AN EXPLORATION OF THE
FAIRNESS DOCTRINE," *INTERNATIONAL JOURNAL OF COMMUNICATION*

[The phrase "public interest"] has acquired a functional and pragmatic definition. It has come to signify that public policy alternative which most deserves enactment. It is, in other words, the highest standard of governmental action, the measure of the greatest wisdom or morality in government.

—FRANK SORAUF,
"THE PUBLIC INTEREST RECONSIDERED," *THE JOURNAL OF POLITICS*

Arguments Against Policy

In some ways, the distinctions between policy (focus on values) and UX (focus on user/profits) mirror the push and pull between government intervention and unrestrained free markets—dynamics that should be familiar to anyone with even a passing awareness of politics. Such debates have been raging for centuries, and they will doubtless continue. On one side, there are thinkers like Ayn Rand, Adam Smith, and Friedrich Hayek, who variously argue that government intervention is unnecessary, or that markets are better able to incorporate the signals and preferences of everyone in society than government can. Thus, such thinkers contend that a laissez-faire approach to regulation is ideal and that the benefits of self-interest have the greatest chance of creating a society that benefits most people. On the other side are those like John Stuart Mill and John Rawls, who posit that applying rules and conscientiously building is the only way to construct a just society.

While this book's bias has been disclosed as being optimistic about the capacity for policy to be a positive force, it's important to acknowledge opposing views. As such, two notable, early public interventions provide fuel for naysayers: railroads and radio waves. The first encompasses the creation of the U.S.'s earliest regulatory body—the Interstate Commerce Commission. With the ICC, Congress declared that all freight and passenger rates "shall be reasonable and just," and outlawed those rates that were not. Here, government was intervening on behalf of the public and in opposition to market forces, which had been driving prices up. The second example is the Communications Act of 1934, in which Congress created a licensing regime for scarce radio wave resources. To justify allocation of this publicly owned resource, Congress declared that broadcasters should operate in the "public interest"—once again placing the public good above the search for profits.

Academics and thinkers who fall more on the "free market" end of views point out the unintended consequences of these policy interventions, and the idea that they may not have actually produced the greatest public good. For example, the railroad intervention led to serious shipping inefficiencies during the first World War, and the radio intervention led to quashing innovation, delaying the introduction of the FM spectrum and (had regulations not been relaxed) stymying the invention of the iPhone.

Quashing innovation is, in fact, one of the main arguments against policy intervention. The "Regulatory Transparency Project," an effort of the conservative- and libertarian-leaning Federalist Society, chronicles side effects of regulation, from environment to emerging technology to health and beyond. Tellingly, their tagline is "Unlocking Innovation and Opportunity." These thinkers consider innovation an unequivocal good.

On the left side of the political spectrum are also thinkers critical of government, like Antonio Gramsci and Paulo Freire. Gramsci's concept of cultural hegemony and Freire's *Pedagogy of the Oppressed* see wide domination of a poor working class by a political and social elite. In their view, systems of oppression are baked into politics through capitalism and class. Both, influenced by Marxism, are pessimistic about the possibility of achieving a just society through existing political systems.

A final argument against government-led policy intervention is a more technical (and less ideological) one—that government simply does not work, or in some cases is not perceived to work very well. Theories for why this is true are many, but they include (to name a few): the undue influence of money in government, which keeps policymakers from answering to the public; the veto power in Congress, which dilutes and complicates bills as they wend their way through the legislative sausage maker; and the confusing interplay between federal/state/local branches of government. These factors, critics say, decrease the frequency and likelihood of government being helpful to the public. They also increase diffuse cynicism toward government in general.

> *While liberals are harmed by the opacity of [government's policy] successes, conservatives are hurt by the inscrutability of its failures.*
>
> —STEVEN M. TELES,
> "KLUDGEOCRACY IN AMERICA," *NATIONAL AFFAIRS MAGAZINE*

Evolving from an Adversarial Stance

Much of the language around regulation of new technologies has historically been adversarial in tone: "battles" or "wars" for control. Indeed, throughout history, regulators have oftentimes come in with a firm hand to take control of perceived excesses. Yet such an adversarial stance is not always the best approach. The public and private sectors can move (and in some cases already are moving) closer together around the emergence of new designs and technologies. To put it simply, designing new technologies that exist in the public interest is much too big a job for any one designer, company, or even simply for the private or public sectors. It must be a collaborative effort between the private and public sectors because of their powerful, complementary lenses.

In reality, business and government do not always exist in conflict with one another, and they have not always been perceived to do so. During the Covid-19 pandemic, as just one example, Operation Warp Speed (2020) was a government effort that assisted private companies in producing vaccines. In times of political polarization, such a partnership might seem unlikely. But throughout American history, we find thinkers with nuanced views on the public-private divide. For example, Supreme Court Justice Louis Brandeis opposed centralization of all kinds, in both capital and government, speaking of "the curse of bigness"—a tradition he inherited from Thomas Jefferson. Just as these thinkers did not take an "either/or" attitude about business and government, there is room for nuance in how policy and the design of new technologies—or the public and private sectors—approach each other as well.

PULLING IT TOGETHER

Both policy and design work on imagining and shaping the world of the future. One does so from the perspective of "values" and the other from that of the "user." While policy can take place in many parts of society, this book's focus will be on government policy, which, in the U.S., primarily is enacted through laws and regulations. Not all people believe that governmental policy can solve problems. But this book is optimistic that by bringing the policy and design perspectives closer together, we are more likely to build a future that reflects the public interest.

Something IS NOT RIGHT...

Proactive **POLICY** Reactive

It's hard to predict the future

BASICS
POLICY & DESIGN

HISTORIC
EMERGENT
HARMS

(NON-DIGITAL)

Present day
EMERGENT HARMS

(DIGITAL)

INTERVENTIONS

Organizations create
their own policy

EXTERNAL
INTERVENTIONS

Government policy
in the digital sphere

Designing WITHIN

POLICY CONSTRAINTS

Bringing
POLICY & DESIGN

Closer Together

Bringing
DESIGN METHODS TO

POLICY CREATION

Enterprise
Design

and

POLICY

WICKED PROBLEMS

and Baby Steps

3

A Brief History of Policy and New Technology

As detailed in the introduction, the concept of "policy" can be applied to solving societal or group problems, whether old or new, from poverty to online abuse. This book is focused on policy as it applies to new designs and technologies as they come into being. It's worth noting that new technologies may overlap with other problem areas, such as education or health, to which policy can also be broadly applied.

This chapter is a sampling of key technological or design developments throughout history, and an explanation of how the policy constraints upon them emerged. The emergence of policy governing digital spheres, specifically, will be covered in Chapter 6, "The Beginning of Outside Regulation." The examples listed here are focused on the United States, with some exceptions for key designs and technologies that emerged in other countries.

The Concept of Harm

"Harm" is a key concept that will be referred to throughout this book. As will be seen, in most cases, policy is developed to address new technologies when harms to the public emerge (that is, a reactive approach rather than a proactive one). In the legal space, the concept of harm is an important one: to seek damages in court, a plaintiff must demonstrate harm and connect it to the actions of a defendant. Legally, harms are placed into "tangible" or "intangible" buckets. Tangible harms, like a physical injury or monetary loss, are easier to quantify and therefore address. Intangible harms, like pain and suffering or invasion of privacy, are a bit trickier to quantify and therefore address.

Threat to the Established Order: Printing

- *Harm type: Intangible*
- *Policy impetus: Threat to entrenched rule*
- *Policy enacted by: Monarchy*
- *Policy type: Licensing requirements, nonjury tribunals, libel laws*
- *Design implications: N/A*

One of the notable early technological advances of the modern world, large-scale printing, emerged at a time of dominance by the monarchy and the church. In this case, the impetus for a policy intervention governing this new technology was the fear of disruption to the established order of rule. Gutenberg's famous movable type consisted of a simple design: cast metal characters that could be rearranged in a frame to mass produce pages of text. In the decades after his press made its appearance, around 1450 in Mainz, Germany, print shops and books exploded across Europe. These presses enabled Martin Luther's book, *The Ninety-Five Theses*, which questioned the corruptions of the church, to reach a much larger audience.

Fearing widespread critique of themselves as well, monarchs kept a close watch on printers. Over the following century, British royalty cracked down on this powerful new tool (that had the potential to foment public unrest) by using some policy methods that are still around today: licensing requirements for printers, nonjury tribunals, and libel laws. Many of these perceived excesses led directly to freedoms enshrined in the U.S. Constitution, including freedom of the press and protections against self-incrimination.

Over the centuries, a more liberal and fundamentally democratic idea of government has emerged: as an entity that exists to serve the interests of the public, rather than protect entrenched power. This means that government has at times tried to navigate the trade-offs between fostering innovation in new designs and tools and preserving the public interest—a difficult balancing act indeed.

A Ground-Up Vision: Coordinating Clocks

- *Harm type: Tangible and intangible*
- *Policy impetus: Evident harms*
- *Policy enacted by: Industry groups and individuals*
- *Policy type: Industry coordination*
- *Design implications: Railroad schedules, watches*

Striking as it may seem, up until the mid-1800s, clocks were not coordinated among cities, and it was the advent of railroads, with their tangible and intangible harms, that led them to be synchronized. Before railroads, when horses were the primary means of transportation, it could take a month to travel between the Midwest and the East Coast of the United States. This meant that people would move between dozens, if not hundreds, of hyperlocal time zones. When railroads emerged, the different time zones led to train collisions and produced a fair amount of confusion for passengers, as they switched time zones so quickly.

The coordination of time as a result of railroads is a noteworthy example because it was not a top-down intervention from government, but rather a decision on the part of the railroad companies themselves, and one dedicated individual in particular who made it happen. The many railroad companies had created an organization called the "General Time Convention," whose job was to coordinate the time schedules of the different trains. The head of that group, William F. Allen, received petitions from both passengers and academics that a wise solution to the confusing and dangerous system of many time zones would be to divide North America into five time zones. It took him about a decade to agree with the approach, but he finally came around.

Allen then engaged in a vast, one-man lobbying campaign, approaching city mayors and heads of various railroad companies across the country. Eventually, he got enough of them to agree to joining standard time, and they set an exact date when the country would coordinate its clocks: November 18, 1883. Interestingly, the federal government disagreed and said that only Congress had the power to coordinate the country's clocks. It took Washington DC until 1918 to declare standard time as federal law. Sometimes, it can take government a while to come around to visionary approaches from a grassroots movement, but that doesn't have to stop the grassroots approach from moving forward.

A Case of Monopoly: Regulating Railroads

- *Harm type: Tangible*
- *Policy impetus: Evident harms*
- *Policy enacted by: Government*
- *Policy type: Regulatory body, antitrust laws*
- *Design implications: N/A*

As railroads grew in economic and social power toward the latter half of the 19th century, they exploited their position to favor certain shippers and ramped-up prices. Congress reacted by creating the first U.S. regulatory body, the Interstate Commerce Commission, in 1887. Congress declared that all freight and passenger rates "shall be reasonable and just," and outlawed those rates that were not, as determined by the ICC.

Additionally, several antitrust laws, including The Sherman Act of 1890, clamped down on railroads and other giant "trusts" like U.S. Steel and Standard Oil. These laws made it illegal for businesses to make agreements with each other that would limit competition, such as agreeing to set prices. The size of large companies, limiting competition to the detriment of consumers, is a theme that continues with big tech today—an idea to be explored in Chapter 6 on the regulation of the digital sphere.

> *Antitrust laws were not put in place to protect competing businesses from aggressive competition. Competition is tough, and sometimes businesses fail. That's the way it is in competitive markets, and consumers benefit from the rough and tumble competition among sellers.*

—FTC.GOV,
THE OFFICIAL WEBSITE OF THE FEDERAL TRADE COMMISSION OF THE U.S.

Clear Physical Risk: Clothing, Toys, and Appliances

- *Harm type: Tangible*

- *Policy impetus: Evident harms*

- *Policy enacted by: Government*

- *Policy type: Regulatory body and design standards*

- *Design implications: Types of materials used, dimensions, testing*

Of all the examples cited so far, the physical risks of consumer goods may need the least explanation for the value of policy intervention. The 1950s saw a flurry of deaths due to consumer goods, and resulted in legislation to address them—notably, the Refrigerator Safety Act of 1956, which was meant to address the deaths of children suffocating in refrigerators, and the Flammable Fabrics Act of 1953, meant to address severe burns and deaths resulting from the synthetic fabric, rayon, used in children's clothes.

The Consumer Product Safety Commission, established in 1972, provides umbrella oversight of such products, rather than what was previously viewed as a piecemeal approach to product safety. From the CPSC's website: "CPSC is committed to protecting consumers and families from products that pose a fire, electrical, chemical, or mechanical hazard…such as toys, cribs, power tools, cigarette lighters, and household chemicals." A study in the *Journal of Consumer Policy* showed that the CPSC had reduced accidental home deaths by an estimated 17,941 over its first ten years of operation.

Today, the CPSC uses a technique called *hazard pattern identification* to issue safety standards for thousands of consumer products. As one example, for cribs, the CPSC did an analysis that found hazards arising from the quality of woods used, paint, the distance of slats, and other factors. This led the organization to issue specific requirements around design and testing to ensure that cribs would be as safe as possible in the future.

The Public Interest: Radio and Television

- *Harm type: Intangible*
- *Policy impetus: Scarcity and fairness, evident and anticipated harms*
- *Policy enacted by: Government*
- *Policy type: Licensing, "public interest" standard*
- *Design implications: Style and delivery of content*

When radio first emerged, it was viewed as a useful tool for rescue operations. Indeed, various ship disasters, including the sinking of the Titanic in 1912, led the U.S. government to mandate that radio equipment be installed in certain ocean-going ships leaving U.S. ports. Within a few decades, another application for this new technology, outside of two-way communication, emerged that had not been anticipated: broadcasting.

Radio spectrum's natural limits, or scarcity, presented two problems: interference over the airwaves and limited access for aspiring broadcasters. The 1927 Radio Act led to the creation of the Federal Communications Commission (FCC). The FCC would become the arbiter of licensure by arguing that any broadcaster should serve the "public interest," just as the Interstate Commerce Commission had. The Radio Act described public interest this way:

> *Despite the fact that the conscience and judgment of a station's management are necessarily personal...the station itself must be operated as if owned by the public...It is as if people of a community should own a station and turn it over to the best man in sight with this injunction: "Manage this station in our interest..." The standing of every station is determined by that conception.*

What exactly "in the public interest" consists of has not been well defined. Given the intangible nature of the harms of radio and television (also under the purview of the FCC), who is to say what is good or bad, right or wrong, to broadcast to the public at large? The FCC has promoted values favoring political balance and disfavoring obscenity, and has considered intervening in the nature of content because of harms cited such as "juvenile delinquency." Similar to the time regulation example, a "grassroots" group (the National Association of Radio and Television Broadcasters) has adopted their own policies for regulating broadcast content, thus keeping serious crackdowns at bay.

A Visionary Crusader: Cars

- *Harm type: Tangible*
- *Policy impetus: Evident harms*
- *Policy enacted by: Government*
- *Policy type: Design standards and regulatory agency*
- *Design implications: Car safety features, testing*

Today, drivers take features like airbags and seatbelts for granted. But cars weren't always designed with these features in place. It was a young lawyer named Ralph Nader who took it upon himself to campaign for automobile safety regulation who made them happen. In 1965, he published a book called *Unsafe at Any Speed: The Designed-In Dangers of the American Automobile*, which detailed problems with brake performance, steering wheels, and crash protection. The following year saw the passage of the National Traffic and Motor Vehicle Safety Act, which required adoption of vehicle safety standards and an agency to enforce them.

The death rate has dropped strikingly, from five deaths for every 100 million miles traveled, to one death for every 100 million miles traveled in 2014. In retrospect, Robert A. Lutz, who was a top executive at BMW, Ford Motor, Chrysler, and General Motors, told *The New York Times*: "I don't like Ralph Nader, and I didn't like the book, but there was definitely a role for government in automotive safety."

PULLING IT TOGETHER

In the days of the printing press, "policy interventions" were a way for rulers to consolidate and protect their power. Over time and with the advent of systems of democratic representation, interventions into new technology morphed into an ideal of promoting "the public interest."

Some key themes from these examples stand out as takeaways, and they will be relevant elsewhere in the book:

- Evident harms are typically required to force a policy intervention—reactive policy is the norm, rather than proactive policy.

- Individuals and industry groups sometimes provide the initial "push" that leads to policy being enacted, and this can take many forms, from a book to a publicity campaign.

- Pursuing policy "in the public interest" gets more difficult as we move into more amorphous, less physical territory. This will certainly be the case as we explore the intangible harms of the digital sphere.

- The consolidation of industries into one or fewer businesses, and the resulting lack of competition, is a recurring theme that results in government intervention.

The preceding examples detail how policy came to be, but not necessarily how it evolved over time. In some cases, notably in the regulation of railroads, a period of deregulation occurred when new forms of transportation, like the automobile and airplanes, undermined the monopoly status of railroads. As is the case in the design world, policy is iterative.

Something IS NOT RIGHT...

Proactive POLICY Reactive

It's hard to predict the future

BASICS
POLICY & DESIGN

HISTORIC EMERGENT HARMS

(NON-DIGITAL)

Present day EMERGENT HARMS (DIGITAL)

INTERNAL
INTERVENTIONS
Organizations create their own policy

EXTERNAL
INTERVENTIONS
Government policy in the digital sphere

Designing WITHIN POLICY CONSTRAINTS

Bringing
POLICY & DESIGN
Closer Together

Bringing
DESIGN METHODS TO POLICY CREATION

Enterprise Design and POLICY

WICKED PROBLEMS and Baby Steps

4

Unconstrained Spaces and the Emergence of Harm

Before policy intervenes in new designs and technologies, think of spaces as being "unconstrained." This is when things are so new that we may not know if or how people will use them and which harms might emerge, so therefore we don't understand which, if any, policy constraints might be needed. As a specific technology gets more uptake among the public and harms begin to emerge, companies and organizations have a choice—they can try to address harms internally (reactively) or ignore them. Despite the efforts of some companies, harms cannot or should not be addressed (only) internally.

That's when external policy constraints, for example by lawmakers, come into the picture. This is the very pattern we'll examine with big tech today—problems that are becoming so tricky and politically sensitive that it is not ideal for them to be addressed by companies themselves (see Figure 4.1).

TYPICAL FLOW of NEW DESIGNS or TECHNOLOGIES

FIGURE 4.1 The flow of new designs or technologies from being policy unconstrained to being policy constrained.

In unconstrained spaces, the design process is quite different than it is in "constrained" spaces. In this chapter, we'll look more specifically at some of the unconstrained spaces of the day—namely, digital design in various forms—and explore what it looks like as harms begin to emerge. Note that digital technology here means systems or resources that create, store, or process data. That includes social media, smartphones, and other devices that use digital technology, such as self-driving cars or smart appliances.

Use Cases: A Singular Focus

The search for use cases—or the question "How can this new technology help solve users' problems?"—is one of the animating forces in design and research of new technologies. As a designer for Amazon's Alexa voice interface, Phillip Hunter was often busy with experiments of just that kind. Years after broad awareness of the interfaces has increased in society, Hunter still says, "We're having a hard time understanding how they're going to be more broadly applicable." In other words, some new idea or tool exists, but how to make it broadly useful can be quite challenging. So designers, engineers, and researchers poke around, sometimes for quite a while, testing out different ideas and designs, until they find one that seems to stick.

> *Designing for emerging technology is very different from designing for established tech. First of all, as technologies mature and gain widespread adoption, core elements of it start to crystallize and solidify. The more they become accepted and known, the harder it is to change them because you have people using them in a certain way or accustomed to certain things. When you are designing for an existing or mature technology along the adoption curve, you have to pay attention to standards or usage patterns. It doesn't mean there isn't room for innovation, but it's more incremental. For emerging technologies, there's this "You don't know yet." If it hasn't been widely adopted or if use case patterns haven't really been established, there's a lot of exploration.*

> —PHILLIP HUNTER,
> PRODUCT AND UX LEADER

Hunter's experience echoes that of Guillaume Chaslot. Chaslot started work as an engineer at YouTube in 2010, perfecting the algorithm for video recommendation, which he had studied in his PhD program in artificial intelligence. At YouTube, he was thrilled to be helping people find content that they wanted to watch—in other words, to find an application for the technology he had studied.

Focused as he was on finding use cases, Chaslot wasn't thinking much about possible negative side effects. As he told producers for *The New York Times' Rabbit Hole* podcast," "I think we were so excited working on this project that we didn't really question too much…We were thinking, yeah, I mean, if people are watching longer, they might be happier about what they're watching." As the podcast series outlines, the "increased watch time" metric actually meant that YouTube's algorithm was feeding users more and more sensational videos—after all, those videos kept people's eyeballs glued to the screen. By some accounts, this then resulted in people becoming increasingly radicalized, and in some cases, full-blown adherents of conspiracy theories around, for example, election fraud and vaccines.

It shouldn't be surprising that Chaslot wasn't considering possible negative side effects of YouTube's recommendation algorithm. For one, such unintended consequences are difficult to predict. And, as discussed, UX focuses in a more granular way on the user and what might bring her "delight" in the moment, rather than bigger picture societal values (which underpin policy). Beyond that, finding use cases is a complicated, time-consuming, and expensive task—so much so that when one sticks, it can override any other considerations a company or practitioner might have. This is particularly true when VC money backing a technological "bet" is expecting a big payday.

Consider the facial recognition company, Clearview AI. Clearview's founder Hoan Ton-That started off wanting to experiment with facial recognition, and he drummed up millions from investors who believed he could create a profitable company with the technology. After trying a number of possible routes, he eventually hit on a formula of scraping social media sites for photos and offering a searchable database to a cadre of willing clients that he perhaps had not initially considered: police departments. Clearview generated controversial headlines in 2020 for such practices. In policy-unconstrained spaces, like facial recognition AI, tech workers are typically driven by the excitement of finding users, that ever elusive "product market fit"—and the underlying monetary need to pay back investors.

DOES THE PROBLEM PRECEDE THE SOLUTION, OR THE OTHER WAY AROUND?

Those who are well-versed in the "fall in love with the problem" ethos of the design process may have had alarm bells go off when learning about the search for use cases in emerging technology. Indeed, this process runs deeply counter to the design dogma of understanding the problem first, and only then crafting a solution that solves it. Instead, in emerging tech, what we often see is a solution in search of a problem. In reality, this is exactly how many new technologies come to be adopted.

In his classic text, *Diffusion of Innovations*, the sociologist Everett Rogers studied innovations in agriculture and other fields. He stated "Does a need precede awareness-knowledge of a new idea, or does such knowledge of an innovation create a need for the new idea? Research does not provide a clear answer to this question as to which comes first." In other words, even this scholar, who dedicated his career to understanding how new technologies enter society, could not conclude definitively whether a new technology (solution) or user need (problem) came first. It's a chicken-and-egg situation where we simply don't know.

Although this pattern is present in the development of much new technology, a classic example of "which came first, the solution or the problem" is represented by the diffusion of email throughout the workplace. Workers in office settings initially widely resisted email and continued to produce work on paper because they were unable to conceive that they had a problem in need of fixing. If those designers bringing email to the workplace had stuck firmly to the "understand the problem first" ethos, email might never have entered our offices.

Emergence of Harm: Harms vs. Pain Points

Designers and researchers who focus singularly on the user's experience are often the first to identify "pain points" and places where they can add "delight." Harm, on the other hand, is not typically something designers are on the lookout for in the course of standard design research (though some things may be both a pain point and harm). Let's take a look at some examples in Table 4.1 to try and understand.

TABLE 4.1 HARMS VS. PAIN POINTS

USER EXPERIENCE	PAIN POINT OR HARM	QUALITIES
A user struggling to submit a form because of a sub-optimally positioned button	Pain point	Solvable by a simple design intervention Identifiable as a problem in the course of standard research Does not run counter to the business goals of the company and therefore is uncontroversial to address
Facebook "outing" a student to her parents before she was ready to tell them she was gay due to unclear privacy settings	Pain point and harm	Solvable by a design intervention May or may not be identifiable as problematic in the course of standard research May run counter to the business goals of the company and therefore be controversial to address
Radicalization of people after watching increasingly sensational videos on YouTube	Harm	May or may not be solvable by a design intervention Individual users unlikely to identify it as a problem (rather it is problematic for "society") and therefore it is not identifiable in the course of standard design research Typically runs counter to the stated business goals of the company and therefore is controversial to address

While the distinctions here may be fuzzy on a case-by-case basis, it is the overarching patterns that are important:

- Pain points are addressable by design interventions, can be relatively easily identified in the course of standard design research, and are usually uncontroversial to address.

- Harms may not be addressable by design interventions, may not be identifiable in the course of standard design research—and may in fact take much longer to "accrue to society"—and can run counter to the stated business goals of a company, making them controversial to address.

Big picture, pain points are aligned with UX (capitalism), and harms are aligned with values (policy).

One designer working "on the ground" and looking for pain points is Jess Dale, a product design manager at an ecommerce company. Her team is focused on fulfillment and meeting the expectations that buyers have around receiving their items. More specifically, they are trying to solve the problem of where in the purchasing journey to set expectations about when an item will arrive, and what impact that has on decisions people make about whether to purchase.

This is a granular focus on one small yet important part of the user experience, clearly connected to the bottom line of the company. Dale says product development teams come to their work with a very focused and specific lens, which doesn't necessarily include looking for harm—"There's a business impact or a financial gain, or from a technical perspective there is a way to operate more efficiently or improve on the infrastructure of how this thing is built." There isn't anyone on her team looking to evaluate the way the system might cause harm. But, like many others in design looking to do good in the world, she believes doing so "would be a truly revolutionary idea."

Anecdotal Harm and Ad Hoc Policy

Let's take a real-world example of a harm that emerged from a new technology—the previously mentioned YouTube algorithm, with credit again to *The New York Times' Rabbit Hole* podcast, which extensively interviewed YouTube CEO Susan Wojcicki. We will return to this example a few times in this chapter, so it's worth understanding a bit of detail about the incident in question.

In 2016, Wojcicki made a decision—which we might call "ad hoc creation of policy"—to override "what users wanted" in favor of a value to society (the underpinning of policy). Wojcicki explained that, historically, YouTube had never seen itself as a platform for news because the platform had no indication that people were interested in it. It was on the occasion of the 2016 Bastille Day terror attack in Nice, France, when 84 people were killed by a truck driving into a parade that Wojcicki made the decision to put news of the attack on the YouTube homepage, despite warnings from her staff that users did not want to see it.

> *I remember that very clearly, because that was the first time I said to them, "You know, it doesn't matter. We have a responsibility. Something happened in the world, and it's important for our users to know." And it was the first time we started using the word* responsibility, *and the fact that we needed to put information in our site that was relevant, even if our users were not necessarily engaging with it in the same way that they would with the entertainment videos.*
>
> —SUSAN WOJCICKI,
> YOUTUBE CEO

Let's break down what happened here. By continuing with the same design that had originally been developed for YouTube—as a place for pure escape—Wojcicki identified that her platform would cause harm to society in keeping people ignorant of a world event. This was not something that users would have identified as a pain point in the course of research. Quite the opposite—they might have said it would be problematic if they *had* been shown the news. In her decision, Wojcicki was choosing a *value* for society over the *profit* that would come from satisfying "user needs." She was implementing an internal policy constraint over the design that had developed for her platform.

Another thing worth noting about this moment is that it happened almost by accident. It wasn't as if Wojcicki went through a rigorous process for quantifying harm, explaining why it was a problem, and figuring out the best intervention for it. In fact, when harms first start to emerge, they are often initially anecdotal moments of "noticing" coupled with sometimes ad hoc interventions.

Take facial recognition. In 2020, we saw stories about *harm to individuals* due to the technology, like the December 29, 2020, article in the *New York Times*: "Another Arrest, and Jail Time, Due to a Bad Facial Recognition Match." The article outlined the story of *one* man who was wrongfully accused of shoplifting and attacking an officer due to a wrong facial recognition match—the third known case of such an incident.[1]

While anecdotes are a critical "canary in the coalmine" moment about more serious and wide-ranging harms, when harms can be clearly named and quantified, the case for addressing them becomes all the more powerful.

Naming and Describing Harms

One place we see many anecdotes about problems—with the same ones sometimes repeated over and over—is in articles and books about privacy. For example, there is the case of the young man who purchased an engagement ring for his fiancée only to have the surprise ruined by Facebook. Or perhaps the woman who learned she was pregnant

---

1. Kashmir Hill, "Another Arrest, and Jail Time, Due to a Bad Facial Recognition Match," *The New York Times*, December 29, 2020, www.nytimes.com/2020/12/29/technology/facial-recognition-misidentify-jail.html

when coupons for diapers arrived at her doorstep. (Target had inferred she was expecting because of shopping habits she had subconsciously changed.)

Privacy is an umbrella concept that has been used to describe such issues, which span today's big tech and the activities of any company that does business online, and hence has data at the core of its operations. Privacy is an important value, codified in the Universal Declaration of Human Rights. Notably, however, the notion of privacy does not necessarily describe *harm* to users. The types of breaches outlined previously are often described with that not particularly useful word: "creepy." The "creepy" word is revealing because it does not necessarily describe a harm; it *feels* wrong.

Now that we have been living online for decades, and with big tech for many years, we are beginning to see harms emerge that are much more pointed than the "privacy" and "creepy" words let on: wrongful imprisonment, spread of conspiracy theories, broken familial relationships, addiction to dopamine, the fraying of democracy, and widespread discrimination along racial and gender lines. Echoing Chapter 3, "A Brief History of Policy and New Technology," with its notions of "tangible and intangible" harms, privacy harms are now becoming more and more tangible. In other words, we have more powerful ways of pointing out harms of digital technology than the "privacy" word has provided.

Lists that actually do quantify today's harms of new technology are many. A couple of notable examples, with many synergies, include Cennydd Bowles' structures in his book, *Future Ethics*,[2] and scholars Danielle Keats Citron and Daniel Solove's "typology of privacy harms,"[3] both of which are shown in Table 4.2.

---

2. Cennydd Bowles, *Future Ethics* (NowNext Press, 2018).
3. Danielle Keats Citron and Daniel J. Solove, "Privacy Harms," (February 9, 2021). *GWU Legal Studies* Research Paper No. 2021-11, *GWU Law School Public Law* Research Paper No. 2021-11, 102 *Boston University Law Review* 793 (2022), https://ssrn.com/abstract=3782222 or http://dx.doi.org/10.2139/ssrn.3782222

TABLE 4.2 QUANTIFYING HARMS OF CURRENT-DAY TECHNOLOGY

CENNYDD BOWLES' LIST OF CURRENT HARM AREAS	CITRON AND SOLOVE'S TYPOLOGY OF PRIVACY HARMS
Discrimination and bias	Discrimination
Addiction and lack of autonomy around digital decisions	Autonomy
	Physical
Lack of autonomy around personal data	Control
Robotics, Internet of Things, and physical risk	Economic
	Reputational
Crime, harassment, and use of AI by law enforcement to control citizens	Emotional
	Relationship
Big tech's contribution to global warming and climate change	Chilling effect
	Thwarted expectations
Loss of employment and increased inequality in the gig economy	Data quality
	Informed choice
	Vulnerability
	Disturbance

Describing harms of emerging technology is no simple matter. It is an undertaking that attempts to describe the story of the world as it is unfolding. So, it can sometimes take a while for what's really going on to come into focus.

> We tell ourselves stories in order to live… We look for the sermon in the suicide, for the social or moral lesson in the murder of five. We interpret what we see, select the most workable of the multiple choices. We live entirely, especially if we are writers, by the imposition of a narrative line upon disparate images, by the "ideas" with which we have learned to freeze the shifting phantasmagoria which is our actual experience.
>
> —JOAN DIDION,
> THE WHITE ALBUM

AI AND FACIAL RECOGNITION: DIFFERENT FROM OTHER TECH?

Recall the Douglas Adams quote from the beginning of the book: "I've come up with a set of rules that describe our reactions to technologies:

"1. Anything that is in the world when you're born is normal and ordinary and is just a natural part of the way the world works.

"2. Anything that's invented between when you're fifteen and thirty-five is new and exciting and revolutionary and you can probably get a career in it.

"3. Anything invented after you're thirty-five is against the natural order of things."

Contrast that with this quote from Woodrow Hartzog, a privacy and legal scholar, in *The New York Times*: "I don't see a future where we harness the benefits of face recognition technology without the crippling abuse of the surveillance that comes with it. The only way to stop it is to ban it."[4]

In 2021, AI and particularly facial recognition, is generating some of the most buzz around a technology that could cause possible future harms (and is causing some now). In China, facial recognition is already used by the government to monitor Muslim minorities in public, ostensibly in order to prevent crimes from occurring. While this may sound Orwellian (the word "facecrime" in *1984* described giving away one's thoughts through one's face), some have struggled to truly quantify and describe the harms—it "might lead to a dystopian future or something," as a hacker quoted in *The New York Times* put it.[5]

4. Kashmir Hill, "The Secretive Company That Might End Privacy as We Know It," *The New York Times*, January 18, 2020, www.nytimes.com/2020/01/18/technology/clearview-privacy-facial-recognition.html
5. Hill, "The Secretive Company That Might End Privacy as We Know It."

Does facial recognition AI—and the broader trends around "surveillance capitalism" as Shoshana Zuboff describes them in her book, *The Age of Surveillance Capitalism*, present a new and novel technological threat? Or will facial AI join television in the pile of tech that people wring their hands about, only to be accepted and normalized later?

Two ideas suggest the former. One is the concept of the exponential pace of the development of technology (see the "Increasing Speed and the 'Pacing Problem'" section of Chapter 1, "A View of the Future"). The specter of Ray Kurzweil's "singularity"—the moment when machine intelligence overtakes human intelligence—may be approaching, and could make today's technological developments categorically different from previous ones. Already, the inscrutable nature of AI points toward this—neural networks draw inferences from so many data points that we can't reverse the algorithm by enough steps to learn much about how they work. In other words, the technology is taking on a "mind" of its own.

The second notion suggesting facial recognition AI may be different from previous tech is that big tech companies themselves, such as Google, have implemented their own internal policies to refrain from using it. In other cases, as with Amazon and Facebook, they have been sued to preemptively stop them from using it. Still, if history, from the printing press to cars, is any indicator, it will take quantifiable harms to emerge before we see lasting and meaningful policy interventions for facial AI.

Documenting and Quantifying Harms

While the individual stories of harm we've discussed are critical for empathy and deep understanding, moving beyond anecdotes is a key step for making the case to intervene. Recall the seatbelt example discussed in Chapter 3. Ralph Nader's book, *Unsafe at Any Speed*, documented at length the safety problems of cars, including brake performance and poor crash protection. It became a bestseller and led to the establishment of the National Traffic and Motor Vehicle Safety Act and its design safety standards for cars. Similarly, we see writers like Safiya Noble in her book *Algorithms of Oppression* or Sara Wachter-Boettcher's *Technically Wrong* documenting harms of today's technology. We'll talk more in Chapter 6, "The Beginning of Outside Regulation," about the emergence of policy in response to the harms of digital tech.

In addition to articles and books for general audiences are academic, nonprofit, and human rights groups studies that quantify harm. One of the earliest groundbreaking studies on the harms of bias in facial recognition AI was 2018's "Gender Shades: Intersectional Accuracy Disparities in Commercial Gender Classification" published by Joy Buolamwini and Timnit Gebru. The paper compared facial recognition systems sold by IBM, Microsoft, and the Chinese company Megvii.[6]

It showed that the systems could accurately predict gender in white men 99% of the time. Meanwhile, for dark-skinned women, their gender was predicted 35% less accurately than it was for white men. The paper laid a foundation for many more studies by researchers and government agencies, and eventually led IBM, Google, and Amazon to state that they would not use facial recognition technology—examples of companies setting internal policy in response to quantified harms of tech, which we will discuss more in the next chapter.

6. Joy Buolamwini and Timnit Gebru, "Gender Shades: Intersectional Accuracy Disparities in Commercial Gender Classification," *Proceedings of Machine Learning Research* 81:1–15 (2018), http://proceedings.mlr.press/v81/buolamwini18a/buolamwini18a.pdf

Other examples include Amnesty International's 2018 report quantifying the harassment of women on Twitter[7] and ongoing research at the UN investigating Facebook's role in spreading hate speech in Myanmar, leading to the Rohingya Muslim genocide. More recently, researchers have shown a correlation between consumption of extreme news on Facebook and the storming of the U.S. Capitol on January 6, 2021.[8] As academics and authors work to quantify harms and publicize them, the case for policy intervention will no doubt become stronger.

Harms That Get Designed in Knowingly

So far we have been talking about harms that "emerge" from new designs or technologies. But sometimes harms get designed in knowingly. An example of this is manipulative designs, or as some governments refer to them, "dark patterns." A definition for manipulative design is: "A user interface that has been carefully crafted to trick users into doing things." Instead of a technology that unwittingly causes harm because its usage is not yet known, manipulative design is knowingly implemented. These include things like making it hard to unsubscribe from a service, or misrepresenting the price of a product.

Company culture can be a predictor of whether manipulative design is used or not. Mike Davidson, former design VP of Twitter, outlined how harm could get noticed and then pointedly ignored by staff. He wrote about an imagined dialogue between two employees at an ecommerce company on his blog:[9]

---

7. *Toxic Twitter—A Toxic Place for Women* (Amnesty International, 2018), www.amnesty.org/en/latest/research/2018/03/online-violence-against-women-chapter-1/

8. Laura Edelson, Minh-Kha Nguyen, Ian Goldstein, Oana Goga, Tobias Lauinger, and Damon McCoy, "Far-Right News Sources on Facebook More Engaging," *Cybersecurity for Democracy* (blog), March 3, 2021, https://medium.com/cybersecurity-for-democracy/far-right-news-sources-on-facebook-more-engaging-e04a01efae90

9. Mike Davidson, "Superhuman Is Spying on You," *Mike Industries* (blog), July 2, 2019, https://mikeindustries.com/blog/archive/2019/07/superhuman-is-spying-on-you

Greg: "Hey, we aren't getting enough people to opt-in to our mailing list when they sign up. Can we try maybe unchecking that box by default but using language such that leaving it unchecked opts people in?"

Desi: "Wouldn't we be intentionally deceiving users if we did that?"

Greg: "Uhhhh, we already add things to your shopping cart that you don't even ask for!"

Desi: "True. This seems like less of a big deal than that. I guess I'm OK with it."

If you've never worked at a tech company before, this is how things go. When faced with making a product decision that is even mildly uncomfortable, employees often first look toward expressed company principles like "Always put the customer first," but the next thing they look for is precedent. What other decisions have we made that look like this one? Designers do this. Engineers do this. Product managers do this. Executives do this. It's an easy way to inform your current decision, and it's also an easy way to cover your ass.

Davidson posits that the "ethical trajectory" of a company is formed in seemingly small decisions like this. If leaders at the company set a less than stellar example, it is likely that such decisions will be continued by staff on the ground. And, even if there were a designer or engineer who felt compelled to be a squeaky wheel and speak up, they could face a potentially hostile environment—because, of course, they would be proposing something that runs counter to the financial interests of the company. In these situations, a "top-down buddy" for that on-the-ground worker is helpful, whether in the form of a leader like Wojcicki, or laws and regulations. We'll talk more about the "top-down buddy" in Chapter 5, "Internal Interventions."

PULLING IT TOGETHER

The current processes for building digital products typically do not include methods for identifying and mitigating harm—for perhaps understandable reasons. Harms are tough to predict ahead of time, in part because some harms only emerge when a product is used at mass scale, rather than beta testing scale. Additionally, the lens of focus for building and testing digital products is on "the user," rather than society. The focus is simply in other places in the capitalist drive to address pain points and find product-market fit.

Nonetheless, harms do begin to emerge in "unconstrained spaces," and they are often noticed and addressed in anecdotal and ad-hoc ways. It can take a while to really grok what's going on with new harms, and even describing them can be difficult before some time has passed. For example, we are in a period where we are only just beginning to understand the true harms that privacy trespasses generate. As more harms of the digital era are understood, academics and writers are documenting and quantifying them, which can generate attention and create an impetus to address them.

In the next chapter, we'll narrow our lens to look at what companies themselves can do as harms begin to emerge to mitigate those negative unintended consequences before external policymaking steps in.

Something IS NOT RIGHT...

Proactive POLICY Reactive

It's hard to predict the future

BASICS POLICY & DESIGN

HISTORIC EMERGENT HARMS

(NON-DIGITAL)

Present day EMERGENT HARMS

(DIGITAL)

INTERNAL INTERVENTIONS

Organizations create their own policy

EXTERNAL INTERVENTIONS

Government policy in the digital sphere

Designing WITHIN POLICY CONSTRAINTS

Bringing POLICY & DESIGN

Closer Together

Bringing DESIGN METHODS TO

POLICY CREATION

Enterprise Design and POLICY

WICKED PROBLEMS and Baby Steps

5

Internal
Interventions

Before external policymaking by government steps in,
"internal interventions," within companies themselves and
in on-the-ground teams, can be attempted in response to the
harms of technology. While this chapter is not strictly about
policy per se, it is about interventions that elevate values and
ethics, which underpin policy, equal to or above the concerns
of private sector user experience, design, and capitalism. We'll
take a look at how companies—or the workers building their
technologies—work to reduce harm before slower-moving outside policy comes into play.

Proactive Mitigation of Harm: Frameworks and Practices

Designers are an idealistic lot. As advocates for users, it can sometimes seem as though they carry the world on their shoulders; in fact, designer and author Mike Monteiro has gone so far as to suggest that the entire world has been "ruined by design." As a result, there is a mini universe of writing and thought on the responsibility of designers to create ethical products. The "ethical" frame is another way of describing the harm prevention we've discussed, with the onus placed more squarely on individuals on the front lines of design.

This book is in part about the limits of what designers can accomplish on their own to create a society that people want to live in. That said, design teams attempting to work ethically *can* be one force for proactively preventing harm before it emerges, particularly when it comes to disproportionate harms. Here are some concepts, frameworks, and best practices for proactively preventing harm through design.

The "Top-Down Buddy"

Recall the imagined scenario from the last chapter of on-the-ground workers discussing whether to design in a dark pattern. Now imagine that one of those workers decides, actually, she doesn't want to design it, but instead wants to speak up. In this scenario, it would be helpful to have a "top-down buddy" for support. For her, a top-down buddy could be her manager or the company CEO. If her manager decides to speak up, the top-down buddy to that person would be the company CEO.

Think of the top-down buddy as a person or entity in a higher position of power who advocates for and supports the lower-level person in their efforts to do something right, even if it runs counter to the financial interests of the company—sort of like a whistleblower advocate (see Figure 5.1). Once you get to the highest levels of a company, there is no top-down buddy within the company to help, and that buddy becomes external—such as a policymaker. A great example is Facebook CEO Mark Zuckerberg. Zuckerberg has been notoriously reticent to implement changes that would lessen his customers' engagement on Facebook, even as engagement has been shown to be correlated with the spread of misinformation and radicalization. Zuckerberg's hesitation is why some people think it is inevitable that Facebook will be regulated by external policymakers. Keep the top-down buddy in mind as we discuss things that on-the-ground teams can do to address harms of new technology.

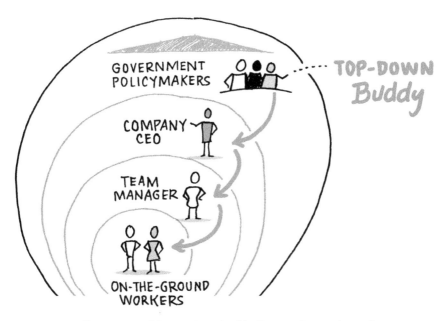

FIGURE 5.1 The concept of the top-down buddy illustrates how authority figures above a given level in a private company can support efforts to elevate values above the search for profit.

Team Diversity and Harm Prevention

In emerging technology of the digital space, we see countless examples of harms that affect people disproportionately based on their identities. A small selection includes wrongful imprisonment based on faulty facial recognition, challenges or outright impossibility of people with disabilities to use computers, and the abuse of women on social media networks.

Many writers have made the case that such harms get designed in because those people building new tech have been primarily able-bodied, heterosexual, young, cisgender, white men who do not or cannot fully consider the experiences of others different from them.

Consider the example of Dr. Frances Oldham Kelsey, a female physician and pharmacologist at the FDA in the 1960s, who refused to authorize the drug thalidomide for treating morning sickness in pregnant women because she felt the research conducted did not confirm it was safe. Kelsey objected to the drug's authorization despite pressure from the manufacturer and the fact that it had already been approved for use in Europe. In the end, her stance prevented an untold number of babies from being born with birth defects. (It is noteworthy that Kelsey has credited her managers for supporting her dissent—she had top-down buddies who gave her objections to the drug's use some credibility and weight.)

In this light, identity and lived experience *in itself* is a kind of expertise that helps designers identify and prevent harm from befalling those most likely to experience it. Diversity and inclusion efforts are therefore more than the "right" thing to do in offering equitable opportunities to all—they are also the smart thing to do because diverse teams have a better chance of making technology that is less harmful for everybody.

Targeting Designs to Those Most Likely to Be Harmed

One method for avoiding disproportionate harms is to target designs specifically to those people most likely to be harmed, rather than some "average middle" persona. Sara Wachter-Boettcher and Eric Meyer have described such an approach in their book *Design for Real Life*, which they term designing for "stress cases"—those people whose identities and situations tend to be ignored. Those cases might include someone with low vision trying to find a doctor's office during an unexpected illness, or someone transitioning their gender presentation. If the design of a maps app were targeted to a low vision person, this does not mean that it would be less usable for someone with high vision—instead, it would be useful for them both.

In other words, designs that target those most likely to be harmed are more likely to work for everyone, including those not experiencing stress or identity related harm. A commonly experienced example involves curb cuts in sidewalks, which were created to help people with disabilities navigate cities, but ended up being helpful for others, such as people pushing babies in strollers. As Ruha Benjamin explains in her book, *Race After Technology*, the benefits of targeting marginalized groups can extend preemptively to help people beyond those groups.

> *In many ways Black people already live in the future. The plight of Black people has consistently been a harbinger of wider processes—bankers using financial technologies to prey on Black homeowners, law enforcement using surveillance technologies to control Black neighborhoods, or politicians using legislative techniques to disenfranchise Black voters—which then get rolled out on an even wider scale.*
>
> —RUHA BENJAMIN,
> *RACE AFTER TECHNOLOGY*

Bringing Users into the Design Process

Another method for avoiding disproportionate harms is to bring users more deeply into the design process—to design *with*, not *for*, as educator and organizer Laurenellen McCann has put it. As Sasha Costanza-Chock writes in their book *Design Justice*, "Design means to make a mark, make a plan, or problem-solve; thus, all human beings participate in design." However, who gets to bear the mantle of "designer" is often rooted in issues of class and race. These notions have been the subject of "Design Thinking and White Supremacy Workshops" by the group Creative Reaction Lab, an online event that was sold out for many months during the Black Lives Matter protests of 2020.

Costanza-Chock and others argue that people usually attempt their own fixes to problems they face, and that designers are typically not the first ones to do so. Thus, swooping in to "solve" someone's problems is not only paternalistic, but also inefficient. In a design justice approach, designers are urged to bring design skills to communities and be led *by* them, rather than bringing users into design spaces to extract their knowledge.

Another reason for designing with users is that there are limits to the empathy that designers can generate without direct lived experience. Designers often attempt workarounds to this lived experience, such as with the tool of personas—flattened "archetypes" meant to describe typical users. Yet without a deeper understanding, designers run the risk of reproducing systems of oppression and harm. As Costanza-Chock states, "Lived experience is non-transferrable." Thus, designers are urged to take that experience into the design process directly by involving people with varied and relevant lived experience to the design problems at hand. These approaches have many flavors and are variously called "participatory design," "codesign," "user-centered design," or "inclusive design."

IS REMOVING BIAS ALWAYS THE RIGHT LENS?

As we have outlined, biases and harms based on identity are a key problem in the digital space. But it's worth asking when bias is the ideal
primary lens through which to consider the impacts of new technology,
and when it might not be.

For example, think about surveillance in public spaces. As we've noted,
facial recognition has misclassified Black people, leading to false arrests.
Now imagine that all bias in facial recognition is fixed—cameras perfectly identify everyone at first glance, and as a result, law enforcement
leaders decide to roll out this infallible system of mass surveillance
to every street corner in the country (a system common in China). As
reporter Karen Hao has put it, "Making face recognition less biased
doesn't make it less scary."[1]

In such a case, removing bias might not be the ideal lens through which to
address this new technology. In fact, companies like Facebook have argu-
ably been using the focus on bias as a red herring to distract from other
key issues. In a detailed investigation of Facebook's use of AI, Hao tried to
probe company leaders on their role in spreading content that led to the
Myanmar genocide. In that incident, members of the Myanmar military
used Facebook to broadcast videos making false claims about the conduct
of Muslims, whipping up ethnic hatred and leading to the murder, rape,
and forced migration of Rohingya Muslims from the country. Rather than
answer Hao's questions about the genocide, Facebook leaders would only
discuss the company's efforts in removing bias from AI.[2]

CONTINUES ➤

1. Karen Hao, "Making Face Recognition Less Biased Doesn't Make It Less Scary,"
   MIT Technology Review, January 29, 2019, www.technologyreview.com/
   2019/01/29/137676/making-face-recognition-less-biased-doesnt-make-
   it-less-scary/
2. Karen Hao, "How Facebook Got Addicted to Spreading Misinformation,"
   MIT Technology Review, March 11, 2021, www.technologyreview.com/
   2021/03/11/1020600/facebook-responsible-ai-misinformation/

CONTINUED ➤

Why do the harms of bias take up so much space and thought at this time? For one thing, problems of bias were some of the first harms of facial recognition AI to be clearly quantified by Joy Buolamwini and Timnit Gebru in their "Gender Shades" study from 2018. These quantified harms have framed much of the thought and effort around AI in the following years.

Showing how something doesn't work for one group while it does work for another group makes a clear case for intervention, as most reasonable people will agree that discrimination is wrong. But in other cases, policy questions center around values that don't have such clear-cut, universal agreement. Consider the use of facial recognition by police. In this situation, we have a value tension of freedom and safety at play. Is it more important to control crime, which police might argue facial recognition helps with? Or is it more important to be free of mass surveillance? The fact that we are dealing with competing values outside of discrimination signals that a lens other than bias might be required for our analysis.

What's more, the focus on removing bias from AI may prevent us from seeing the forest for the trees in wider, structural issues of discrimination. In the example of a perfectly functioning system of mass surveillance, it is likely that Black people and other minorities would suffer disproportionately in other ways, and perhaps even more severely, than if the bias of the AI were not removed in the first place—something we see happening with the Uyghur minority in China now. "If it doesn't work well, it's bad. If it works perfectly well, it's still bad, depending on how it's used," as Timnit Gebru has said. We live in a deeply unequal society where benefits and harms are always unevenly distributed. It is important to find the right lens through which to consider impacts and not miss the wider issues at play.

Imagining the Future

Engineers and others working on new technology do sometimes run exercises to try to determine where a project might go south. A commonly used tool that originated with the U.S. military is the Failure

Mode and Effects Analysis (FMEA). One could imagine an automobile engineer using this tool to determine the failure effects of a punctured tire, for example. The engineer would simply think through a number of possible failures, the impacts on the user, and mitigating actions to take. However, this tool does not necessarily think through unintended consequences when the technology *does* work as intended. As we've been discussing with the case of AI, this type of future prediction is a bit more challenging.

Still, tools exist to help stretch the imagination. Cennydd Bowles outlines several of these in his book, *Future Ethics*. One such tool is the futures cone, which is a framework invented by Joseph Voros for considering different outcomes for the future: the possible, plausible, probable, and preferable (see Figure 5.2). By thinking through each of these layers, designers might think through how to steer toward the "Preferable."

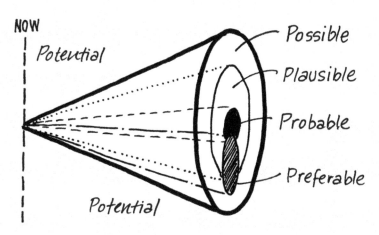

Source: Joseph Voros, a generic foresight process framework (2003)

FIGURE 5.2 The futures cone is a framework for stretching the imagination to think through impacts of new technologies.

Another tool is the futures wheel, which places a new tool at the center of a diagram (say, deep fakes), and then charts out a ring of "first-order" consequences around it, a ring of second-order consequences beyond that, and so on. As Bowles puts it, running a futures wheel exercise with a tech team "isn't about accurate prediction so much as opening a team's eyes to possibility." The outcomes of such an exercise could shape the decisions that a team makes now.

Eli Pariser, of Civic Signals, advocates for an approach of "thinking in terms of what to aspire to, not just what harms to stop." An in-depth research project, Civic Signals took insights from the design of physical public spaces, such as parks and libraries, and proposed several tenets, or "signals," for designing healthy digital spaces—things like "encourage the humanization of others," "strengthen local ties," and "show reliable information."

Proactively Baking in Values

Just as Civic Signals advocates for thinking aspirationally about what we want, rather than what we don't want, a number of frameworks exist for proactively baking in values to many stages of the design process. This notion exists at the value-specific level and also in a more general frame of thinking through values. For example, the value of privacy has a number of frameworks associated with it. One of those is the Privacy-Aware Design Framework proposed by author and designer Vitaly Friedman, which embeds the value of privacy into various aspects of digital design, including forms, cookie consent, and notifications. Another value with frameworks associated is that of justice. Design justice advocates for a design framework that works toward the value of justice, which can mean giving more attention to groups that have been previously marginalized or left out of design processes.

Value sensitive design, pioneered by professors Batya Friedman and David Hendry, is a broader approach that does not identify one single value, but rather attempts to embed thinking about values at every phase of the design process. The approach promotes asking explicit questions about which values designers, stakeholders, and users hold, and which value tensions might emerge by the introduction of a new design into a specific context. Value tension is an issue that has emerged in big tech as large companies grapple with questions around, for example, safety and censorship.

> *In technical education, students might pursue design and engineering projects in a largely value-neutral manner. However, technical projects, along with the tools and technologies they produce, are not value-neutral. To the contrary, tools and technologies make some goals easier to obtain and others harder, support some human experiences and values but not others.*
>
> —DAVID HENDRY,
> *DESIGNING TECH POLICY*

> *Our choice is not between "regulation" and "no regulation." The code regulates. It implements values, or not. It enables freedoms, or disables them. It protects privacy, or promotes monitoring. People choose how the code does these things. People write the code. Thus the choice is not whether people will decide how cyberspace regulates. People—coders—will. The only choice is whether we collectively will have a role in their choice—and thus in determining how these values regulate—or whether collectively we will allow the coders to select our values for us.*
>
> —LAWRENCE LESSIG,
> *"CODE IS LAW"*

Social Science Research and Harm Prevention

As we've explored, there are things that design teams can do to anticipate or prevent harm. But there is a case to be made that expecting design teams to take on the full responsibility for harm prevention adds yet another job on top of what is an already demanding day of work within a capitalist ecosystem. Think about it: designers, engineers, and product people in the private sector must concern themselves with how their work helps the company's bottom line. They need to think about usability, the technology that runs the thing, and adapting as new competition enters their market. It's a lot. So, some companies have decided that they need people on staff whose entire job is to look for harms and who are trained to do so.

Sam Ladner has a PhD in sociology and is a social scientist at Workday. She is asking questions about possible unintended consequences that product teams aren't typically set up to ask. As she explains, "Most frequently in UX research, we don't do social science research, we just do usability testing—asking, does this robot work? While I would ask, will this robot kill us?"

Most tech companies, other than perhaps the largest, do not have dedicated researchers like Ladner on staff. Whether they have never considered that they need such positions, or that such people are actually good at what they do, and can "gum up the works" for companies, may be contributing factors. One example is Timnit Gebru, the AI researcher who was fired from Google in 2020 over a paper that investigated some of the risks of working with large datasets on natural language processing. The paper noted that AI models could be used to generate misinformation about, for instance, a pandemic or an election, and could be problematic when doing machine translation, which has led to at least one false arrest. When you consider that Gebru's earlier research on bias in facial recognition led several companies to preemptively stop using the technology, perhaps it is not surprising that Google sought to discredit her research. After all, such research might stop them from using other new tech whose harms are not yet well understood—or prove that the company could have prevented harms that emerged later on down the line.

Reactive Responses to Harm

Would the proactive approaches outlined earlier solve all problems of harmful design? While they are likely to have some impact, notably around bias and disproportionate harms, they are unlikely to solve all problems of emerging technology. As noted, many harms accrue at a "societal" level, rather than an individual one, and can take a longer time frame to become clear. Thus, as history shows, most external policy is created in response to "evident harms," once they become concrete and quantifiable. It's likely that reactive responses to harms of new technology will always be needed. The following examples are some of the types of reactive responses currently seen internally within companies and organizations.

Design Features for Harm Reduction

One obvious site of abuse and harassment—or evident harms—in the digital world is Twitter. Mike Davidson, former VP of design there, led efforts to try to mitigate that harassment. While it's important to note that many users, notably women and gender nonconforming people, still see Twitter as a site of abuse (and there are efforts to create alternatives, such as the app Block Party), Davidson's efforts are worth examining for their attempts to intervene in quantifiable harms.

Davidson notes that when the platform first launched, abuse was a problem, although not hugely widespread because there simply weren't that many people on it. Once Twitter grew, the company was better able to quantify the abuse. Davidson credits Del Harvey, Twitter's head of trust and safety at the time, with pointing out that once you get into the hundreds of millions of tweets, even if one out of every 10,000 tweets is abusive, that's still a lot of tweets. Twitter couldn't moderate every single tweet before it went live, so Davidson's team asked themselves how they could allow people to protect themselves?

> *The first thing we built was the block button, where people can't see your tweets at all. That helped because it put friction between the abused and the abuser, but it wasn't perfect because you could open an anonymous browser window, or create a fake account. The other thing that wasn't good about block is that it's visible to the abuser that you've done something. So imagine you're a woman and your ex-boyfriend is harassing you on Twitter. You use the block button. Your ex-boyfriend sees that as an act of aggression. We needed an opaque way to do this so the abuser didn't know that they had been muted. If I've muted you, the abuser doesn't know. You think you're yelling at me, and I just can't hear you anymore.*

—MIKE DAVIDSON,
DESIGN AND RESEARCH LEADER

The team settled on both "block" and "mute" as capabilities for protecting against abuse, in addition to the ongoing work of the policy team working to block accounts (more on internal policy teams later in this chapter).

Importantly, Davidson points out that many people working on Twitter had never experienced the kind of abuse they were trying to solve for. "I don't know how it feels. I can try to put myself in the head of someone who has experienced that, but there's no substitute for that," he says. This hearkens back to the *proactive mitigation of harm*—the power of diverse teams, bringing users into the design process and targeting designs to those most likely to be harmed. While all of these methods could have impacted Twitter proactively, they could also be helpful when designing reactively. The Twitter mute button is just one of countless design responses to harm in the digital world, from better forms that collect less user data, to optical recognition that recognizes all skin pigments.

Worker-Led Movements

In several tech companies, workers have organized to push their employers to reduce the harm of their products. Perhaps most notably, at Google, hundreds of workers have participated in walkouts and formed a union. They have protested both workplace issues and strategic technology decisions, including the development of artificial intelligence technology for use by the Department of Defense. In fact, they have connected the two subjects: in noting the firing of Timnit Gebru, Google employees pointed out that "unfair workplaces create unfair platforms."

These movements are significant when considering the "top-down buddy" concept. When support is not forthcoming from the top for lone whistleblowers, workers have banded together, a bit like a union, to be their own "buddy" and create a force formidable enough to deal with the power that their employers hold. While we will be talking about external, governmental policy constraints in the upcoming chapter, some believe that internal, worker-led movements like Google's may be the most effective method of addressing harms of new tech.

Internal Policies and Policy Teams

As noted in Chapter 2, "Policy and Design Basics," policy can emerge in markets, government, and in civil society. Private sector companies certainly have policies of their own. Kristina Podnar details in her book, *The Power of Digital Policy*, that companies have differing policies and policy maturities, depending on their size, age, and specific needs. While Podnar suggests that companies can create proactive digital policies, most tend to do so in response to some problem that arises, such as a lawsuit.

CURRENT FOCUS AREAS FOR INTERNAL POLICY TEAMS

A sampling of Kristina Podnar's comprehensive list of suggested official policy areas, from her book, *The Power of Digital Policy*, is outlined here. Most of these are areas that contain established law that could pose a legal risk for companies. Others encompass emerging technology that could pose a reputational or legal risk down the line.

- Accessibility
- Advertising (paid, social network, grassroots)
- Algorithm formatting and management (AI)
- Analytics and metrics collection
- Blockchain
- Children's online privacy protection
- Content ownership and management
- Cookies and tracking
- Copyrights and protections
- Data breach response
- Data privacy
- Data localization
- Digital fundraising and donations
- Digital risk financial statement
- Email marketing and spam
- End-user-generated content
- Health information and the Health Insurance Portability and Accountability Act (HIPAA)
- Online piracy
- Product advertisement and placement
- Supply Chain Act and Modern Slavery Act
- Technology identification and selection
- Virtual and crypto currency

As policy teams exist now, they largely interpret laws that are already on the books, and ensure that a company is in compliance with them. In other words, they act primarily as risk managers for known and agreed harms (although it's noteworthy that Podnar urges companies to see policy as opening opportunity by providing guardrails, as well).

Before laws exist for certain harm areas, we see companies developing policy in an ad hoc fashion, in response to problems as they arise, as noted in Chapter 4, "Unconstrained Spaces and the Emergence of Harm," in the YouTube example. Another good example of this is the ad hoc bans of former President Donald Trump from both Twitter and Facebook in response to the January 6, 2021, insurrection at the U.S. Capitol. Although there had been many calls to ban Trump from these platforms before January 6, once violence erupted, the harm became concrete enough for the companies to take action, ad hoc as it was.

When Internal Policy Teams Aren't Enough

The question of Donald Trump being banned from Facebook is an example of the limits of what internal teams can accomplish—either proactively or reactively. Whether to keep Trump off the social network was an issue so thorny that Facebook set up its own "supreme court" to try to adjudicate it (and other tricky issues). Although Trump had violated the platform's policies prior to January 6, Facebook had maintained his presence because, as the president, the platform had deemed him "newsworthy." When his presidency ended and Joe Biden took over the presidency, the court—called "The Oversight Board"— was tasked with determining whether it would let him back on the platform or maintain his suspension.

The Oversight Board is modeled on actual courtrooms, and it deals in "cases" and "appeals." It is unsurprising that the need for what amounts to internal company law has arisen for Facebook and other large tech companies as well. In some cases, these companies are as powerful or perhaps even more powerful than nation states themselves. As such, they are being forced to confront the very same issues that policymakers do—what are our values, and what type of world do we want to create?

In many cases today, large tech companies are being forced to weigh seemingly conflicting fundamental societal values, such as safety (keep Trump off Twitter) and freedom (let Trump say whatever he wants, wherever he wants). This is no simple undertaking. Some observers have posited that private companies should, in fact, not be making such decisions, and that they should be decided by leaders democratically elected by people. Now that we've looked at proactive and reactive *internal* interventions, we'll turn our attention to *external* interventions, where the "top-down buddy" becomes government policy.

PULLING IT TOGETHER

Before external policy intervenes, companies can attempt their own internal interventions to harm. These can include both proactive mitigation of possible harm and reactive responses to evident harm. As issues get thornier, some companies' internal interventions begin to resemble the systems of law in government that exist to resolve the most difficult value tensions in our society—thus paving the way for "external intervention" by policymakers themselves.

Something IS NOT RIGHT...

Proactive **POLICY** Reactive
It's hard to predict the future

BASICS
POLICY & DESIGN

HISTORIC EMERGENT HARMS
(NON-DIGITAL)

Present day EMERGENT HARMS
(DIGITAL)

INTERVENTIONS
Organizations create their own policy

EXTERNAL INTERVENTIONS
Government policy in the digital sphere

Designing WITHIN **POLICY CONSTRAINTS**

Bringing POLICY & DESIGN *Closer Together*

Bringing **DESIGN METHODS** TO **POLICY** CREATION

Enterprise Design and **POLICY**

WICKED PROBLEMS and **Baby Steps**

6

The Beginning of Outside Regulation

Now that we've looked at what companies can do internally to try and address harms, we turn our attention to what outside regulation, or government policy, looks like. While Chapter 3, "A Brief History of Policy and New Technology," covered how policy has historically emerged outside the digital space, in this chapter, we'll look more specifically at the regulation of digital technologies and the internet, figure out how the current landscape has come to be the way it is, and ponder where it might go next as calls to rein in big tech and address new threats continue.

While this chapter cannot be a comprehensive history of the regulation of all digital technology around the world, it will use salient examples to try and paint a broad picture, with a focus on the U.S. and issues around "big tech." As a reminder, we are defining digital technology as systems or resources that create, store, or process data, which includes things like smart appliances and social media.

The Digital Technology Government Policy Landscape

Recall discussions of where government policy "takes place" from Chapter 2, "Policy and Design Basics": this includes regulations (issued by regulatory agencies) and laws (which go through lawmakers and the legislative process). These basics of government policy apply to technologies of the digital space as they do to anything else. The key regulatory agencies with purview over the internet in the U.S. are the FTC (Federal Trade Commission) and the FCC (Federal Communications Commission). Meanwhile, laws that govern digital technologies exist at both the federal and state levels. There is much debate about whether this setup makes sense, and there have been calls for new agencies to be established to adjudicate emerging technology. But as things stand in 2022, the foregoing description encapsulates the U.S. landscape.

Note that the laws for digital technology can overlap with other domain-specific laws of society (see Figure 6.1). Thus, a new healthcare app would need to be sure that it complies with the FTC's guidelines around not misleading consumers online. But it would also be subject to HIPAA laws pertaining to patient privacy. Also note that laws and regulations can overlap at the geographic level. So, while the GDPR (General Data Protection Regulation) protects user privacy for members of the EU, the online privacy of California consumers is protected by the CCPA (California Consumer Privacy Act). For online companies that operate globally, as many do, these geographic differences can present a complicated landscape because the same systems often need to be built differently in different places to comply with a variety of laws and regulations.

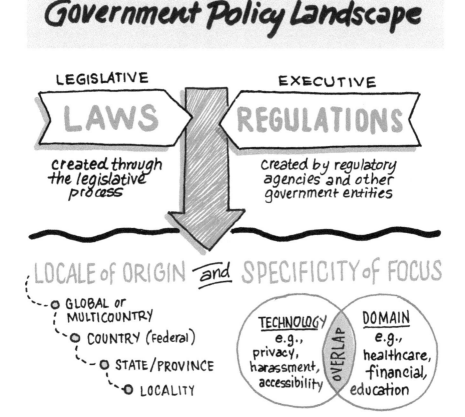

FIGURE 6.1 Government policy of the digital technology landscape includes both laws and regulations. Each of these varies by geography as well as specificity of focus.

THE FISHBONE DIAGRAM: A POLICY ANALYSIS TOOL

A tool that some policymakers may use in their analysis for how to intervene in a societal problem is the Ishikawa Diagram, otherwise known as the
"Fishbone Diagram." Figure 6.2's diagram is a way of identifying the problem
to be addressed and drilling down to various possible places for intervention.

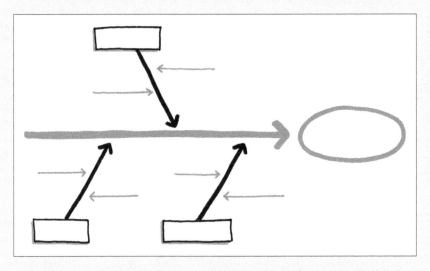

FIGURE 6.2 The Fishbone Diagram is a tool for analyzing the root causes of a
given problem.

On the right side of the diagram is the main problem that policymakers
are hoping to impact, ideally associated with a numerical metric that can
be measured. The boxes indicate primary causes of the problem, and the
"bones" are sub-causes. There may even be yet further sub-sub-causes
branching off the bones.

By using an Ishikawa Diagram, policymakers can decide which underlying causes they want to intervene in to impact the problem. As an example, to impact low participation in U.S. elections, policymakers may decide, after deeper analysis, that intervening in civics education in schools will have the biggest bang for their buck on impacting the outcome (or problem) on the right. See Figure 6.3. One could imagine using the fishbone diagram to try to address a problem of digital technology, such as increasing adherence to conspiracy theories.

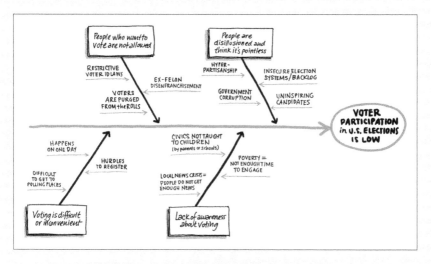

FIGURE 6.3 Policymakers could choose to intervene in any of the causes or sub-causes in order to impact the problem of low voter participation in U.S. elections.

Enforcement and Interpretation of Policy

In general, both regulations and laws work by penalizing those who run afoul of them. For regulations, government agencies can issue fines or file enforcement actions for breaches of their policy, which can result in the entity in question paying a settlement, or being forced to fundamentally restructure their products. For laws, individuals have the right to sue by demonstrating harm. Or, an attorney general, as part of the executive branch at either the state or federal level, can bring a suit simply because an entity broke a law. Lawsuits can end up in a courtroom and can also result in a fine or the subject of the lawsuit being forced to change its behavior.

The role of the judicial branch (courts) is to interpret laws and apply them to individual cases. Courts are an important piece of the policy puzzle because of the concepts of "statutory law" and "common law." Statutory law encompasses the text of a law as written, while common law is law that has been developed on the basis of preceding rulings in court cases. In essence, laws are made up of more than just their text; they are also colored by precedent in previous court cases that pertain to them. Thus, the legal landscape is constantly shifting and changing shape as new judgments are issued.

Factors That Have Advanced Digital Tech Policy

How laws and regulations come to be is a complex process without a single reliable pattern. Many different forces impact policy formation, such as politicians in power and their backgrounds and priorities, court cases, the regulatory bodies in question, historic events, media coverage, and the presence of lobbyists influencing decision makers. Still, it's worth noting some key factors that have led to the adoption, or at least introduction, of digital tech government policy, as these factors may point the way to future developments.

Guidelines and Best Practices

Outside of government, there are nonprofits and standard-setting bodies that have led the way toward policy, or thinking around policy, in the digital sphere. By operating outside both government and the private sector, these organizations can impact the thinking of both. W3C (World Wide Web Consortium) and IETF (Internet Engineering Task Force, part of the Internet Society group) are two of the main organizations that set standards for the web. W3C has produced WCAG (Web Content Accessibility Guidelines) among many other standards. WCAG, introduced in 1999, issued 14 guidelines and 65 "checkpoints" for making the web accessible, such as "Provide equivalent alternatives to auditory and visual content." While there is no legal requirement to adopt WCAG in the U.S., doing so helps organizations steer clear of lawsuits that could be brought under the ADA (Americans with Disabilities Act).

Internet Society and IETF produce reports, standards, and policy recommendations aimed at spreading access and increasing the speed and reliability of the internet globally. Internet Society has produced an Internet Impact Assessment Toolkit, which is intended to help policymakers and others determine whether regulations or other forces could alter the fundamentals of the internet and lead to harmful consequences, primarily around what it sees as core values of universal accessibility, openness, and decentralization.

> *While the Internet's critical properties cannot guarantee the associated benefits, together they form the necessary condition for future evolution in a way most likely to create and disseminate the value that comes from connection.*
>
> —INTERNET SOCIETY

Creative Commons is another organization that aims to shape guidelines for the web independently, outside the legal sphere. Essentially, CC has issued guidelines for policy around copyright. It allows creators online to voluntarily use various "flexible" copyright symbols, proffering more rights for other online creators to remix and reuse. In all of these examples, independent organizations can influence thinking around legal or policy concepts by experimenting with "outside-the-box" ways of operating.

Publicizing Harms

Documenting, quantifying, and publicizing harms (covered in Chapter 4, "Unconstrained Spaces and the Emergence of Harm"), which can attract the attention of lawmakers and regulators, has had an impact on the introduction of government policy over digital technology. Researchers and whistleblowers have helped to publicize and leak known harms, including bias in algorithms and false arrests, the damaging impact of social media on teenage girls, the decline of democracy, and even genocide. Drawing the attention of lawmakers to these issues has had a direct impact on the introduction of policy, such as the Filter Bubble Transparency Act (to be discussed later in this chapter).

Connecting with Regulatory Agencies

Regulatory agencies learn about breaches of rules through a number of avenues, including research and fact finding, through the course of supervisory duties, and notably through direct contact with whistleblowers. As an example, in 2020, the children's online learning program ABCmouse was found guilty of trapping unknowing subscribers into recurring payments on its online platforms. Then-FTC Chair Rohit Chopra put out a call for designers to provide evidence of manipulative patterns in order to find other such breaches and enforce the rules against them (see Figure 6.4).

Rohit Chopra ✔️
@chopracfpb

The @FTC needs to combat dark patterns so we can contain the spread of digital deception. If you are a designer concerned about dark patterns or wish to be an informant, please file a confidential complaint with the FTC or contact my office. ftc.gov/system/files/d…

12:46 PM · Sep 2, 2020 · Twitter Web App

FIGURE 6.4 Then-FTC chair Rohit Chopra sought to connect directly with designers to learn about manipulative patterns.

ABCmouse agreed to pay $10 million to settle the charges, which the FTC said would be used to provide restitution to its victims. The FTC may even implement a whistleblower reward, aimed at employees of big tech companies who report privacy breaches, which would provide a portion of recovered funds to whistleblowers themselves. Such incentives have proven successful in other venues, such as at the Securities and Exchange Commission's (SEC) rewards for reports of investment advisor fraud and insider trading.

Public Whistleblowing

While the previous example concerns on-the-ground workers connecting with government from behind the scenes, whistleblowing can also take place in a more public sphere. Consider the case of Frances Haugen, the former Facebook product manager who in 2021 collected troves of internal company documents and leaked them to the press. The resulting articles proved that Facebook knew of many harms in its products, including its impacts on teenage girls' self-esteem and its promotion of radical political ideas. Haugen employed a strategic approach, first developing a relationship with a reporter at *The Wall Street Journal*, which resulted in a series called "The Facebook Files," and then delivering the documents to a wider journalistic audience.

This approach then led to more interviews and even testimony before Congress. Haugen's stated intention was to get enough attention to prompt government action.

> *Facebook has demonstrated they cannot act independently. Facebook, over and over again, has shown it chooses profit over safety. It is subsidizing…it is paying for its profits with our safety. I'm hoping that this will have had a big enough impact on the world that they get the fortitude and the motivation to actually go put those regulations into place. That's my hope.*
>
> —FRANCES HAUGEN,
> PRODUCT MANAGER AND DATA ENGINEER
> IN AN INTERVIEW WITH *60 MINUTES*

Planting Seeds for Mental Models

Since predicting the future impacts of new technology is difficult, people tend to fit possible harms into existing frameworks and ways of thinking. This has certainly been the case with privacy, as it forms one of the overarching concepts for trying to understand the harms of digital technology.

How privacy emerged as a key concept to understand harms online—and how to address them—dates back to the 1970s with the work of an engineer and writer named Willis Ware. Ware was deeply concerned with the mass collection of human data and what that might mean for rights and freedoms. His writing (among other forces and historical influences) informed regulations that would come down the pike many decades later.

> *Most of us have suffered at least the annoyance of having to cope with a computer-based system that, outwardly at least, appears not to care how it has mistreated us or, worse, has given false impression or subjected us to harassment. It is, of course, true that the computer per se is not the culprit; rather the system*

*designers have, for whatever reasons, seen fit not to create
humane systems that are considerate of the data subjects about
whom information is held. Thus, in the struggle to protect the
personal privacy of the citizen, the preferred solution would
adjust the balance of power between citizen and record system
in such fashion that **the individual has both opportunity
and a mechanism to contest, correct and control personal
information held about himself.** [emphasis added]*

—WILLIS WARE,
"RECORDS, COMPUTERS AND THE RIGHTS OF CITIZENS," 1973

A notable piece of Ware's privacy framework was the idea that people should have "control" over data collection practices. We can draw a line between this and both U.S. and European privacy legislation, which mandates that users must give consent for how their data will be used—in other words, it gives users control. To gain that consent, we see the now-ubiquitous cookie pop-ups on many parts of the web (which have been criticized and may be walked back). The point is that it is always a good moment to put forth concepts and frameworks for thinking about new technologies. Powerful ideas that take root may come to fruition years later.

Key Government Policy Approaches to Digital Tech Today

How is government presently attempting to shape policy around digital technologies? There is not one single approach, but rather the problem is being addressed from a number of angles, including the dominance of online platforms, to data practices, to the application of "real world" laws, to the digital sphere. It will be interesting to see which of these approaches may have the most impact, or perhaps which combination. Following are some themes of the public sector approach to shaping digital technologies.

Privacy Rules

Drawing at least partly from Ware's early ideas, privacy is one of the key areas where government policy attempts to impact digital technology and the internet. Much of the business model of the internet today is based on the usage of massive amounts of consumer data, which author Shoshana Zuboff has termed "the surveillance economy." Privacy regulation aims to reign this in.

One of the landmark pieces of government policy over digital tech is the EU's GDPR (General Data Protection Regulation), which went into effect in 2018. Among other things, this regulation requires consumers to have control over their data, just as Ware counseled in his writings, and it imposes hefty fines for breaches. The largest fine to date was issued in 2019, for €50 million ($61 million dollars) against Google for a breach of transparency rules. Other localities have followed the lead of the EU, including the state of California with its CCPA (California Consumer Privacy Act).

More broadly, however, the U.S. lags behind in its lack of general privacy regulations. The FCC, which regulates communications by radio, television, satellite, wire, and cable across the U.S., and the FTC, which is charged with protecting consumers, could both make the case for taking on responsibility around privacy. Both have brought privacy breach cases against companies ranging from Google, to brick and mortars, to ISPs. In the absence of more wide ranging regulation, however, this piecemeal approach toward privacy in the U.S. is likely to continue.

Protections for Online Platforms

Debates over freedom of speech online can be seen to center around Section 230 of the Communications Decency Act. Passed in 1996, Section 230 essentially gave online platforms immunity from liability for the content that others published on them. This legislation has purportedly allowed online platforms to flourish without fear of legal action. Section 230 has been challenged a number of times in court, and today the immunity is not unlimited, requiring providers to remove content related to child sex trafficking and copyright violation. Unlike other laws and regulations cited here, section 230 provides *protection*, rather than punishment. In Chapter 8, "Bringing Policy and Design Closer Together," we'll review some new approaches to regulation that are less about top-down enforcement.

Bans on Specific Practices

The informed consent inherent in many privacy frameworks puts the onus on users to control data practices of large companies—in other words, users tell companies what they can or can't do. Bans, on the other hand, remove that issue altogether by prohibiting certain practices of large companies in the first place. The Banning Surveillance Advertising Act is a bill that, if passed into law, would prohibit certain segmentation and targeting of ads based on personal data.

Beyond advertising, there have been calls for bans of emerging technology before their implications are better understood. Facial recognition and drones are some current examples. In 2022, the IRS walked back plans to introduce facial recognition into its tax filing process after objections from legislators and civil rights groups. While not an official ban, it signals the reticence of lawmakers to see this technology's use expanding in society.

> *There's not a pressing need for most new digital technologies. Some innovations, of course, are almost completely positive: anesthesia, electric light, radio, vaccines. But today's society often celebrates innovation for its own sake, even when the benefits are questionable…Is it really worth a crowded, buzzing sky filled with drones to get one-hour delivery of consumer goods, instead of delivery in 24 hours, or even two days? Is virtual reality so great that children should, effectively, grow up*

with their eyes glued to video screens?… These types of innova-
tions repeatedly fail to provide overall improvements in truly
meaningful ways, like how deeply people love each other, how
compassionately people care, how well society supports the less
privileged, or how wisely humans steward the planet.

—KENTARO TOYAMA,
COMPUTER SCIENTIST AND RESEARCHER

Antitrust and Anticompetition

While, as of 2022, the U.S. Congress has been in partisan gridlock for many years, the size and power of big tech companies seems to be one cause with the potential to unify lawmakers across the aisle—after all, the dominance of these companies calls into question the power of the political system as a whole. Antitrust laws emerged in the 1800s in response to monopolies in several industries, including steel and oil, whose dominance had led to higher prices and lower quality for consumers. Such antitrust laws, and later, the creation of the Federal Trade Commission, were ways for government to foster a fairer marketplace, and consequently, better products and services for consumers.

Today, small businesses and users operate online in a world of massive tech centralization with a preponderance of walled gardens, which can be seen as the modern parallel equivalent to the monopolies of a previous era (look no further than the different colored bubbles between an Android user's and iPhone user's messages). Using antitrust rules and anticompetitive legislation could likewise help attack the dominance of big tech companies and ostensibly create benefits for users in the process. However, whether breaking up big tech would result in better services for users is a matter of debate. Antitrust can create cheaper services, but what impact will that have when services are already free?

On the internet…prices are low and every service dreams of scaling to a billion users. The internet is an ecosystem of high-quality, low-or-no-cost goods, with substantial openness and readily available access.

—CHRIS RILEY,
GLOBAL INTERNET POLICY AND TECHNOLOGY RESEARCHER

Applying Existing Laws to Digital Harms

Existing laws provide frameworks and recourse for some new harms of technology—but not all. For example, harassment, copyright, and accessibility are all areas of harm that are currently covered by existing laws that could be extended to the digital sphere. But many others are only just being enumerated and understood. As a result, we tend to see prosecution not of harms to users explicitly, but rather practices against *investors* with shareholders suing under the charge of securities fraud (securities fraud basically alleges that a company did something bad and didn't immediately tell shareholders about it). Securities fraud was brought against Facebook in the Cambridge Analytica scandal, in which Facebook data was used in political targeting. In essence, securities fraud allows prosecutors to go after public companies for lying to investors, rather than what they might have done to users.

And so contributing to global warming is securities fraud, and sexual harassment by executives is securities fraud, and customer data breaches are securities fraud…In a world of dysfunctional government and pervasive financial capitalism, more and more of our politics is contested in the form of securities regulation…When you punish bad stuff because it is bad for shareholders, you are making a certain judgment about what sort of stuff is bad and who is entitled to be protected from it.

—MATT LEVINE,
BLOOMBERG OPINION COLUMNIST

THE BEGINNING OF OUTSIDE REGULATION · 87

What are the harms of the digital sphere that we might want govern-ment policy to address better, but which it's not set up to do now? Some examples include autonomy harm and relationship harm. A per-son's autonomy over their own choices can be diminished because of algorithmic recommendations. And relationships among families and friends are being negatively impacted by the preponderance of disin-formation and conspiracy theories online. Key challenges here are that many online harms become evident much later than they are "perpe-trated," and accrue to society rather than individuals.

Recall the discussion around "pain points" vs. "harms" in Chapter 4. Just as UX focuses more granularly on the experience of individu-als, so do courts; people must show a harm to themselves to have the capability to sue. The individualized harm frame of our system may be ill-suited to more collective harms emerging from new technology.

> *Courts struggle with privacy harms because they often involve future uses of personal data that vary widely. When privacy violations do result in negative consequences, the effects are often small—frustration, aggravation, and inconvenience—and dispersed among a large number of people. When these minor harms are done at a vast scale by a large number of actors, they aggregate into more significant harms to people and society. But these harms do not fit well with existing judicial under-standings of harm.*
>
> —DANIELLE KEATS CITRON AND DANIEL SOLOVE,
> LAW PROFESSORS AND PRIVACY SCHOLARS

Transparency

Calls for big tech companies to be more transparent about their practices are one proposed approach to curbing the impact of online harms. The thinking is that if the mechanics of content and ad targeting are revealed in plain language, users can begin to understand how they are being manipulated—and even demand different services, pushing companies to change their practices. The Filter Bubble Transparency Act would mandate such disclosures, granting the FTC new powers of regulation. The impetus for this bill came mainly from whistleblower revelations about the harms of Facebook, one of the "contributing factors" mentioned previously.

> *Facebook and other dominant platforms manipulate their users through opaque algorithms that prioritize growth and profit over everything else. And due to these platforms' monopoly power and dominance, users are stuck with few alternatives to this exploitative business model, whether it is in their social media feed, on paid advertisements, or in their search results.*

> —DAVID CICILLINE,
> HOUSE REPRESENTATIVE FOR RHODE ISLAND'S 1ST DISTRICT

Changes over Time

As understanding of harm evolves, based on factors like the ones cited in this chapter, governmental approaches will no doubt change and new ones will appear. The dominance of big tech may be successfully challenged in the future, at which point, other harms and technologies will take the spotlight.

To understand how these changes occur over time, it's illuminating to think back on digital tech–related laws of a previous era. In 2012, in response to perceived harms of digital technology, laws called "SOPA" (Stop Online Privacy Act) and "PIPA" (PROTECT IP Act) were proposed. As their names suggest, the laws were meant to protect intellectual property and creative outputs on the internet. A huge uproar and coordinated protests took place, alleging that the laws would effectively destroy the open and sharing nature of the internet. These protests led lawmakers to rescind their support for the laws, and they did not pass.

It is interesting to note that at the time, a government crackdown on the internet was perceived by many as evil and wrongheaded (in fact, Google was one of the coordinators of the protests). Meanwhile in 2022, the opposite—government's *lack* of crackdown on big tech—is seen as a failure. As researchers, scholars, designers, and engineers work to understand and illuminate the harms of digital technology, how policymakers propose to intervene could flip yet again, in ways we cannot yet perceive.

PULLING IT TOGETHER

Many factors have contributed to policy of the public sector that addresses digital technology. Designers and others concerned with building tech can take lessons here, and consider documenting and publicizing harms, publishing thought leadership, or proposing guidelines of their own that then become more diffuse throughout society.

The ways that government is intervening in digital tech today include ideas ranging from antitrust measures to privacy laws to bans—and these notions are evolving. Just as design is iterative, so is policy. As harms are documented and publicized, and new ways of thinking emerge, governmental attention and approaches will shift, and we will see other ideas for shaping the digital world we live in.

Something IS NOT RIGHT...

Proactive **POLICY** Reactive

It's hard to predict the future

BASICS POLICY & DESIGN

HISTORIC EMERGENT HARMS

(NON-DIGITAL)

Present day EMERGENT HARMS

(DIGITAL)

INTERNAL INTERVENTIONS

Organizations create their own policy

EXTERNAL INTERVENTIONS

Government policy in the digital sphere

Designing WITHIN **POLICY CONSTRAINTS**

Bringing POLICY & DESIGN Closer Together

Bringing DESIGN METHODS TO POLICY CREATION

Enterprise Design and POLICY

WICKED PROBLEMS and Baby Steps

7

Design in Policy-Constrained Domains

New tech of the digital space has often been characterized by Facebook CEO Mark Zuckerberg's "move fast and break things" ethos. The notion of "permissionless innovation"—exploring without boundaries or constraints—has been advocated by many thinkers. But in several domains of our society outside the purely digital, harms have been well quantified, and policy is mature enough to constrain them. Designing in these policy-constrained spaces is significantly different than the "exploratory" feel of designing for new technology, such as the example of design for voice interfaces described in Chapter 4, "Unconstrained Spaces and the Emergence of Harm."

In this chapter, we'll examine what it's like to design in three domains that are already constrained by policy—construction, healthcare, and finance—and what lessons we might take from designers in those spaces (see Figure 7.1).

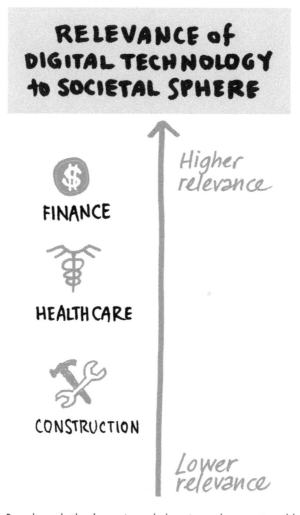

FIGURE 7.1 Based on whether harms in each domain can be more tangible or intangible, finance, healthcare, and construction are more or less relevant to digital technology.

It's important to note that, even though many harms in these domains are understood, policy in all of them will always be evolving. This evolution may be in response to societal or political changes, or perhaps the emergence of new technologies. In fact, all of these spheres intersect with digital, and as such, they are changing. Think of the innovations in these domains as the "outer edges" of the domain—in finance, cryptocurrency is a good example of innovation at the edges, whereas traditional banking is a more established part of the domain. The outer edges, where innovation happens, are often lacking in policy.

In Chapter 3, "A Brief History of Policy and New Technology," we discussed tangible and intangible harms; in the legal space, harms are placed into "tangible" or "intangible" buckets. Tangible harms, like a physical injury or monetary loss, are easier to quantify and therefore address. Intangible harms, like pain and suffering or invasion of privacy, are a bit trickier to quantify and therefore address. By that token, each domain we'll look at is more or less relevant to the digital, based on how relatively tangible or intangible their harms might be—and thus is more or less lacking in policy.

With its solid grounding in the material world, construction has the least relevance to the digital domain; healthcare is more relevant with its connection to the human body, records, and privacy concerns; and finance is the most relevant to the digital space, given that money can be completely physically intangible, and therefore highly digital. This relative scale can give us a sense of how much digital technological innovation exists and thus how relatively lacking in policy the various domains are—the more relevance to the digital, the more the technological innovation, and thus the more unconstrained the "outer edges" of the domain will be.

Designing in the Construction Domain

Building codes and laws are ancient, although they have evolved significantly over the centuries. In perhaps the oldest building code known to humanity, the Old Testament addresses the flat roofed "four room houses" typical of the Iron Age. Obviously, if a flat roof were constructed with no railings, someone could easily fall from it. Deuteronomy 22:8 thus states: "When you build a new house, make a parapet around your roof so that you may not bring the guilt of bloodshed on your house if someone falls from the roof."

New Threats and Centralization

While some harms were obvious as far back as 2,000 BC, others only became apparent later. For example, in 1906, the Great San Francisco Earthquake prompted an updating of building and fire codes. Today, threats of climate change—including energy efficiency needs, increased fires, and flooding—are prompting a further review of codes.

Another notable evolution in building codes is the consolidation of many disparate local codes into unified ones under central groups. This progression is common in several parts of the world. In the U.S., for example, disparate local codes were scrapped in favor of the IBC (International Building Code), which is issued by a group called the International Code Council. U.S. municipalities can choose to adopt these "model codes" and most do so, modifying them for their local needs. The EU uses a regulatory framework for all its member states called "Eurocodes."

In both cases, countries outside the areas in question use these centralized codes; for example, Russia and Turkey both use Eurocodes. Perhaps it's unsurprising that construction knowledge has become more and more unified over the years; after all, what minimizes harm in one earthquake prone zone is likely to do so in another. It may be that, with more time, the entire world will be unified under a standard building code, sharing the collected knowledge of centuries.

Coming Around to the Code Review

Given the extensive constraints imposed by construction codes and regulations, architects often start projects with a process known as a "code review," familiarizing themselves with any zoning ordinances for the area, local laws, and such. For architects just starting their careers, who are focused on building something beautiful, this may feel like a limiting or annoying process. But more experienced architects understand that these constraints can be helpful.

Carina Bien-Willner, an architect based in Los Angeles and Tucson, confirms as much. The "parameters," as she calls them, can make for a successful project for many reasons, whether it's the safety of the inhabitants or the overall look of the neighborhood. "The whole point of architecture is building for humanity, for people. You can't do that in a vacuum. If you do, it almost isn't architecture anymore, it just becomes art," she says. "You don't want to build a project and have everybody hate it, and you want it to be structurally sound." Architects need to learn quickly how to be creative and make meaningful work within the parameters of the building codes in a way that doesn't take away from the project.

When Policy Is Prescriptive

Whether because of shifting values, world events, emerging research, or new technology, policy continues to evolve, and that includes the field of construction. In the city of Los Angeles, citizens have long been concerned with the process of "mansionization," which involves the construction of large, boxy houses that extend to the property line. This restructuring of the house sizes is changing the character of historic neighborhoods in ways that some see as undesirable (see Figure 7.2).

FIGURE 7.2 A newer, boxy home built close to the property line in Los Angeles, next to an older, smaller home.

As a result, the Los Angeles City Council issued an update to the city's zoning codes called the "Baseline Mansionization Ordinance." The problem, as Bien-Willner states, is that the policy dictates the design in far too much detail: "It may be true that we have too many big boxes in the city, but now we're going to have boxes with exactly the same angles." She would have preferred that the policy dictate the desired outcome, and allow designers to figure out the precise solution (see Figure 7.3).

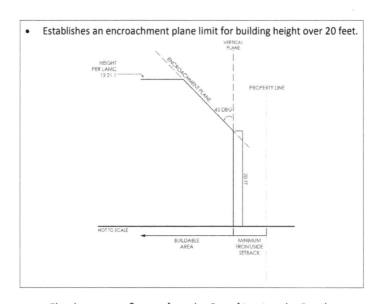

FIGURE 7.3 This design specification from the City of Los Angeles Baseline Mansionization Ordinance prescribes in detail how to build in a way that achieves certain policy goals.

Bien-Willner and her team were brought into the policymaking process, but only at the very end, when their voices held little weight. She believes that having professionals, as well as concerned citizens, involved earlier would have led to a better result. As we'll see, the difficulty of getting key stakeholders in the room to form policy is one of the major challenges of doing it well.

Designing in the Healthcare Domain

Moving on from the construction example, which is so firmly rooted in the material world, we turn our attention to designing in the healthcare domain. This domain is also rooted in the physical, as it pertains to the body, but healthcare overlaps with the digital more than construction does, at least at this point in time (perhaps in the future the built environment will be "eaten by software" as well). In part, this has to do with the centrality of patient records in the healthcare process, which naturally entails issues of privacy and access. The digitization of healthcare is wide ranging and vast, encompassing everything from telehealth and big data to communications and electronic health records. All of these changes—not to mention the need to improve healthcare as a whole—mean that healthcare policy continues to constantly evolve.

Complexity and Subject Matter Expertise

Every domain of practice requires some amount of subject matter expertise. Architects go to school to acquire it in their field, but digital designers don't always have specific training to learn the ins and outs of their particular domain. Aris Blevins, a UX designer at Epic Systems, didn't have training in healthcare before he started his job. Epic is, by most measures, the maker of the largest Electronic Health Records (EHR) software in the U.S. So Blevins, and other new joiners, are required to take the first three to six months of the job for a "mini college course" in healthcare history, policy, and more. The training may have sub-specialties for specific areas like oncology or pediatrics.

Even with that extensive onboarding, the people in the weeds of building software are not expected to stay abreast of every policy nuance and change coming down the pike. So Epic employs specialists who keep their eye on these developments, inform their teams when they need to know of changes, and are available "on call" to answer questions that might come up in the course of product development. "If you're working in this domain, you better have regulations be part of what you do, or you'll have major failures and oversight that will cost you," Blevins says.

Balancing User Needs and Policy Requirements

Blevins works specifically on tools for doctors to use in the clinical setting. It's not always easy to design in ways that both meet the needs of these users and stay within regulatory bounds. An example of that is requirements around numbers that physicians need to be shown when they are reviewing results from blood tests. While physicians would just like to see the basic test result number they are looking for, they are also required to be shown a reference range, collection time, and the lab that did the work. This contextual information helps make more sense of that main number since not all labs do blood tests the same way.

Like Bien-Willner, who has learned to get creative within her parameters, Blevins also says, "We're getting more clever about things. I think what's useful is, once you understand what those requirements are gonna be, you can start to dive in and talk about—what if we use other design elements as a factor, like time for example?" Blevins and his team have been experimenting with a hover state for the contextual information so they do not provide doctors with an overwhelming amount of information initially. On these design decisions and others, his team will lean on their on-call policy experts to ask, "Are we hitting the right balance? Is this still being safe?"

Impacting Policy from a Design Perspective

Epic is a big enough company, and has enough high-ranking employees, that they actually have a line into policymakers and can give their two cents on decisions that are coming down which could impact their software—although they don't always succeed. A policy decision many software and healthcare providers had concerns about was the 21st Century Cures Act, which included a mandate that patients be able to access their entire health record. While physicians worried that patients might have too much information, and not enough relevant information to make sense of, the mandate went forward and will have impacts on many aspects of EHR software.

Blevins is chair of a group called EHRA (EHR Association), which brings together designers of EHR software and, among other things, tries to impact and interpret policy decisions. He recently convened a summit to talk through physician notes and how they interface with updated billing codes, which insurance companies and the Centers for Medicare and Medicaid use to bill for healthcare services—a complex space. They wanted to ask "What makes a good note in this new environment?"

While it took countless volunteer hours to organize physicians and EHR vendors, only once they were all in the room did they realize they were missing at least a couple of key groups—billing and compliance professionals—who could help provide a full picture of the space. "Building these bridges is a hard problem," Blevins says. "It's a space that's so dense, deep, and multivariate that it's easy to get wrong. How do you get enough representation from all the people who have a hand in the healthcare pie? You can't talk to them separately. It becomes this infinitely large problem of time, coordination, and vetting of the right people."

Designing in the Finance Domain

The financial landscape is a good example of a domain that continues to evolve as new harms emerge. Some of the earliest monetary systems—as far back as 2,000 BC—included rules for interest and repayment. Fast forward a few millennia, to 2009, and the global financial system nearly collapsed because of its overexposure to mortgage-backed securities. Resulting legislation led to increased oversight of financial institutions and new governmental agencies.

On top of the constant policy evolution that happens as a result of real-world events comes the entrance of fintech on the scene. Because of its aforementioned disconnection from the physical world, and the centrality of record keeping, finance's overlap with the digital is just as broad ranging, or possibly even more so, than healthcare tech. In the world of digital money, the landscape is rapidly evolving across payments, lending, retail banking, and market investments in deep and overlapping ways, like a plaid fabric pattern, and designers bump into regulation in interesting ways.

Building in Friction

Much like healthcare, finance is a space where mistakes carry a high cost. Alex Kirtland, VP of UX at Goldman Sachs says, "It's not unusual to hear stories about some poor trader who clicked the wrong button and got themselves fired because they clicked 'buy' when they meant to click 'sell.'" In 2020, a Citibank employee notoriously lost the bank nearly $900 million when repaying the wrong amount to creditors. As a result, there are requirements around building in friction to the user experience—forcing users to confirm an action over multiple screens, for example.

This approach runs counter to dogma in the UX space like "don't make me think," bring "delight," and create "frictionless" experiences. Karen Pascoe, Head of Digital Design Innovation at Wells Fargo, says, "I have at times made experiences too fast, too seamless, and too effective that it has been necessary to put a seatbelt in." The payments space in particular is one where she believes the user needs "cognition" to avoid errors. And, as we'll see, the trading space is one where mistakes carry quite a high cost.

Friction also enters the banking experience in the need to collect a large amount of customer information. This is a result of KYC or "Know Your Customer" laws, which require banks to verify user identity to prevent fraud and money laundering. In this and the previous examples, designers might get creative to balance the potential for user frustration with rules that exist to prevent harm.

At the Edges of the Domain

Even with the rules that do exist, designers may find themselves at the edges of the finance domain, where regulators haven't yet reached. This is more common in the startup space than it is at established banks, where multiple regulatory agencies provide oversight, stringent reporting requirements exist, and regulatory constraints are "baked in" to the design process. (Kirtland points out that designs at Goldman Sachs go through a hefty legal review before being released into the wild.)

Consider the example of the fun and easy-to-use trading app, Robinhood. Robinhood has made trading so simple and accessible that it has lured in tens of millions of users. Inevitably, some of these investors will be inexperienced, like 20-year-old college student Alexander Kearns. After seeing a negative balance of $730,000 on Robinhood, Kearns committed suicide in 2020, asking in his suicide note that "How was a 20-year-old with no income able to get assigned almost a million dollars' worth of leverage?" See Figure 7.4.

FIGURE 7.4 Robinhood's "digital confetti" celebrates when users make trades.

Robinhood is an example of new tech where the drive for users and profit that underpin design, and the values at the core of policy, are at odds with each other (revisit Chapter 2, "Policy and Design Basics," for a refresher on these underlying drivers). The average person makes money in investing by holding their investments for long periods of time. Robinhood, on the other hand, makes money each time a user trades. Their platform therefore promotes behavior that runs counter to their users' long-term interests. The gamification of their UX reflects this, urging users to make trades over and over. While in the short term users may find this experience delightful, in the long term it will be anything but.

Karen Pascoe points out that financial companies in the headlines for exhibiting bad behavior have all failed to embody a key value they should abide by: trust. While, as previously mentioned, more established banking companies have regulations built in to try and ensure that trust (granted such regulations do not always succeed), newer companies are figuring out the ethics, or values, around their products on their own. In these spaces, where Pascoe says you may be "trailblazing ahead of regulators' understanding of the medium," it's important to understand both the letter, but also the spirit of regulations, and build in trust to products. This echoes the "internal policy interventions" discussed in Chapter 5, "Internal Interventions," and the concept of proactively baking in values where such concepts do not yet exist. If Robinhood had proactively baked in the value of trust to its platform, they would likely have a very different user experience, and, quite possibly, a different business model.

PULLING IT TOGETHER

Reflecting on the construction, healthcare, and finance domains, some themes recur. Depth of knowledge—and up-to-date knowledge—is required to design well in complex, regulated domains where policy continues to evolve. Designers in policy-constrained domains must be extremely creative to balance user needs with policy rules. And finally, designers can impact policy, although it's tough to convene everyone needed, at the ideal moment, to have a good outcome. In Chapter 8, "Bringing Policy and Design Closer Together," we'll further explore the last point—of designers impacting policy—in more depth.

Something IS NOT RIGHT...

Proactive **POLICY** Reactive

It's hard to predict the future

BASICS
POLICY & DESIGN

HISTORIC
EMERGENT
HARMS

(NON-DIGITAL)

Present day EMERGENT HARMS

(DIGITAL)

INTERNAL
INTERVENTIONS

*Organizations create
their own policy*

EXTERNAL
INTERVENTIONS

*Government policy
in the digital sphere*

Designing WITHIN
POLICY CONSTRAINTS

Bringing
POLICY & DESIGN
Closer Together

Bringing
DESIGN METHODS TO
POLICY CREATION

Enterprise
Design
and
POLICY

WICKED
PROBLEMS

and Baby Steps

8

Bringing Policy and Design Closer Together

How can government move upstream in the technology design cycle, look at new tech, and analyze how it could impact the world? How might the policy and design spheres collaborate productively? How can we make reactive responses to tech harm as proactive as possible?

We've talked a fair amount about various ways that design and policy approach each other. Now let's turn our attention to an idea bubbling in a number of ways: bringing the policy and design spheres closer together in a more intentional and proactive way. Think of this happening a bit like a zipper—two sides start far apart and then weave closer together.

This metaphor does not presume that bringing policy and design closer together is a neat way of "solving" the challenges of emerging technology. But doing so could present better ways of bringing new things into the world.

> *The goal of foreseeing the future exactly and preparing for it perfectly is unrealizable… The future can't be predicted, but it can be envisioned and brought lovingly into being. Systems can't be controlled, but they can be designed and redesigned.*

> —DONELLA MEADOWS,
> ENVIRONMENTAL SCIENTIST AND SYSTEMS SCHOLAR

Governmental Analysis of New Tech

Policymakers in the U.S. Congress have long understood the need to keep an eye on emerging science and technology issues. They were perhaps best equipped to do so between 1974 and 1995, when the Office of Technology Assessment (OTA) was functional within Congress. The office existed to "provide early indications of the probable beneficial and adverse impacts of the applications of technology and to develop other coordinate information which may assist the Congress."

The office advised Congress on issues ranging from computers to vaccines, but was defunded in 1995 after Republicans took control of the House and Senate—and just as the internet was taking off. It is interesting to ponder what the office might have analyzed—perhaps social media, deep fakes, or privacy issues—had it continued. Today, Congressional capacity and expertise for analyzing new technology has significantly diminished, according to a 2019 study by Harvard University's Belfer Center. There is often a lack of science and technology expertise among congressional staff, high staff turnover means that knowledge gained leaves quickly, and the increased pace of technological change also contributes to this decreased capacity. Over the years, many have advocated for the re-establishment of the OTA, including former presidential candidate Andrew Yang. And others, including former FCC Chair Tom Wheeler, have called for a stand-alone agency to broadly regulate the internet and digital technology.

> *Between two extremes lies the view of those who recognize that benefit and injury alike may flow from technology, which, after all, is nothing more than a systematic way of altering the environment. They recognize that the quality of life has been greatly improved by technological advance and would deteriorate rapidly in a period of technological stagnation. . . . The choice, from this perspective, is not between the abandonment of technology as a tool of human aspiration and the uncontrolled pursuit of technology. . . . The choice, rather, is between technological advance that proceeds without adequate consideration of its consequences and technological change that is influenced by a deeper concern for the interaction between man's tools and the human environment in which they do their work.*
>
> —FROM A 1969 REPORT BY THE NATIONAL ACADEMY OF SCIENCES AS CONGRESS WAS CONSIDERING ESTABLISHING THE OTA

Which new technology areas should government focus on in its analysis? An interesting proposal is to look at trends in VC spending and use that as a gauge for which technologies are coming down the pike and should get a closer look from lawmakers. In their paper, "Regulation Tomorrow: What Happens When Technology Is Faster Than the Law?"[1] authors Mark Fenwick, Wulf Kaal, and Erik Vermeulen counsel that if certain tech areas—say, artificial intelligence or drones—were seeing an infusion of early stage venture capital, it would be time to start taking a look, before such tech got to later stages. Such approaches

---

1. Mark D. Fenwick, Wulf A. Kaal, and Erik P. M. Vermeulen, "Regulation Tomorrow: What Happens When Technology Is Faster Than the Law?" *American University Business Law Review*, Volume 6 Issue 3 (2017), https://digitalcommons.wcl.american.edu/cgi/viewcontent.cgi?article=1028&context=aublr

may help government policymakers and designers of new tech move closer together at earlier stages of development (see Figure 8.1).

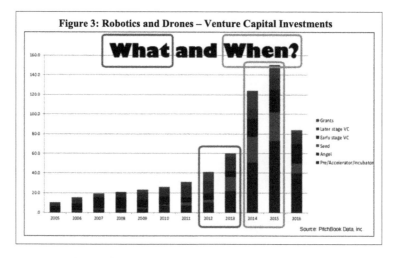

FIGURE 8.1 Collecting data on various tech areas, such as robotics and drones, and analyzing when different types of investments, such as seed, angel, or late stage VC, can give an indication about when to start examining given fields.

Bringing Tech to Government, Bringing Policy to Tech

Efforts are afoot to increase the capacity of Congress, in order to understand the development of technology. TechCongress is an example—a nonprofit-backed fellowship that places skilled technologists with members of Congress. B Cavello is one of those. They previously worked at the Partnership for AI, developing resources for guiding ethical development of AI. Cavello often ran into a wall where AI practitioners would duck calls to implement guardrails that could curtail emerging or possible harms of the tech. Instead, the practitioners would point to policymakers, saying it was *their* responsibility, or that things wouldn't change until there was a legal requirement around it. So Cavello decided there had been enough talk about policymakers' responsibility, and decided to join them to try and guide ethical implementation of new technology from within Congress, entering the fellowship in 2021.

On the flip side, efforts are in place in some institutions to educate technologists on the policy process. Aspen Institute and its Tech Policy Hub do just that, having trained over 150 people. By imparting knowledge of how regulations and laws are shaped, the hope is that these people with previous expertise in technology will go on to impact public policy. For example, fellows have addressed the abuse of elders online, government procurement, and Covid-19 responses in some of their work following the program. Other programs, such as the Tech Talent Project and Coding it Forward, attempt to bridge the policy-technology divide.

Designers and Researchers Influencing Policy Agendas

While policy evaluation is an existing, robust approach to assessing policy impact, designers and other technologists outside of government who understand user experiences are, in fact, well-positioned to opine on policies that could make a difference. That's partly because they are on the front line of harms that emerge from new tech, able to perceive them quickly, and can examine them at their own speed. Laura Edelson, a PhD in computer engineering at NYU, basically scans for new harms of the internet by studying online disinformation systems. Her work, and those of others like her, has been called the "critical community," and having a line from such deep, on-the-ground work to policymakers could influence how tech policy is shaped.

In the healthcare space, Juhan Sonin is a designer with opinions on policy as well. Sonin is the director of GoInvo, a 12-person design studio focused specifically on healthcare. While he and his team pay the bills by designing everything from patient workflows to small apps, their "side work" (or perhaps their more central work) concentrates on trying to impact policy from their vantage point on the ground.

The team has a list of around 50 problems in healthcare, such as "errors are the 4th leading cause of death" and "prices vary," and they rank them according to a rubric including outcomes to patients and money spent (see Figure 8.2). Sonin is working on building coalitions throughout the public and private sectors to attack some of these top policy positions. There is no concrete payday for Sonin with this policy advocacy. Instead, he says "We pour the measly profit we make at the design studio back into this work and that's how we fund it."

☐	Title	Details	Spending
4	Errors are 4th leading cause of death	Behind heart disease, cancer and COVID-19. These errors include patient misdiagnosis, incorrect prescription of a drug or procedure, and hospital based infections. Most people will be subject to at least one diagnostic error during their lifetime. These errors often go unreported.	$750,000,000,000
5	Spending is wasted	25% of healthcare spending is wasted on failure of care delivery, failure of care coordination, over-treatment or low-value care, pricing failure, fraud and abuse, and administrative complexity.	$935,000,000,000
6	Prices vary	Based on your insurance plan and health care facility, the price of an intervention can vary by as much as 65%. This is because the rate for every service is negotiated between payers and providers. Medicare prices are closest to the actual costs of care.	$235,000,000,000
7	Preventive care is prevented	This leads to both health and economic impact. When preventive care is not prioritized, patients get sicker, end up having to pay more for their care, and in a lot of cases, die. Economic productivity decreases when patients need to take time off of work to address preventable illness.	$260,000,000,000

FIGURE 8.2 Sonin's website, ushealthcareproblems.com, ranks the top problems in U.S. healthcare, according to his agency.

Regulatory Sandboxes

Regulatory sandboxes are a tool that has been employed since 2016 specifically in the world of fintech, although the concept could have wider application beyond it. The idea is that new financial services firms "enter" a government sandbox—an environment with relaxed rules where they run monitored experiments for a predefined period of time. This allows the firms to assess the impact of their designs on customers, while also gaining guidance from regulators on which rules might apply to them.

Sandboxes have been touted as a way to promote innovation while reducing regulatory burdens. However, a report from the World Bank assessing 73 sandboxes in 57 different geographic areas also suggests that the sandboxes have value for regulators: they help fill in gaps in needed financial regulation, and help regulators develop deeper expertise around fintech trends and areas that may need their attention. The results of sandboxes in the fintech world are mixed—some of them have yielded a few long-lasting policy results, while others have not provided the desired information to policymakers. It may be that designing a realistic testing environment is so complicated that it makes a proper experiment challenging.

Collaborative Policymaking

Some amount of collaboration is already built into the process of rulemaking by regulatory agencies, through the "Notice of Proposed Rulemaking"—when a new regulation is about to be passed—and the "Advance Notice of Proposed Rulemaking"—earlier on, when an agency is just starting to think about a new rule. When this process kicks off, anyone, from members of the public to private companies, can provide feedback. Companies that have a stake in the outcome of rules can employ members of an in-house policy team to keep an eye out for such notices and participate in them. For example, when the CFPB (Consumer Financial Protection Bureau) issued an Advance Notice of Proposed Rule Making on Consumer Access to Financial Records, the fintech company Plaid responded with their inputs to the forthcoming rule. (See Figures 8.3a and 8.3b.)

Yet, is the exchange of lengthy documents truly the best approach? Some scholars have questioned it, advocating for more genuinely collaborative, workshop-style approaches to solving big problems. Similar to Aris Blevins, the designer at Epic from Chapter 7, "Design in Policy-Constrained Domains," who tries to bring interested parties to the actual table, scholars Judith E. Innes and David E. Booher have also called for such messy collaboration in the formation of policy.

Innes and Booher cite the example of California water policy as a venue where such an approach was successful, with environmental, business, agriculture, and local government organizations building a strategy and procedures for managing the limited water supply in northern California's semi-desert.[2] They suggest that such a collaborative approach would work in other policymaking sectors of society as well. As we will explore in Chapter 10, "Enterprise Design and the Policy Space," facilitation is indeed one of the key missing skill sets in complex enterprise spaces attempting to solve big problems.

> *To achieve collaboration among players with differing interests and a history of conflict, the dialogue must be authentic, rather than rhetorical or ritualistic...Most of us are so unaccustomed to authentic dialogue in public situations that to create and manage it typically requires the help of a professional facilitator and special training for participants. Stakeholders have been accustomed to concealing their interests and engaging in positional bargaining rather than in discursive inquiry and speculative discussion or interest-based bargaining. They tune out those with whom they assume they disagree rather than explore for common ground.*

> —JUDITH E. INNES AND DAVID E. BOOHER,
> PROFESSOR OF PLANNING AND POLICY EXPERT

2. Judith E. Innes and David E. Booher, "Collaborative Policymaking: Governance Through Dialogue," in *Deliberative Policy Analysis*, ed. Maarten A. Hajer and Hendrik Wagenaar (Cambridge University Press, 2003), www.csus.edu/indiv/s/shulockn/executive%20 fellows%20pdf%20readings/innes%20and%20booher%20collaborative%20 policymaking.pdf

Interoperability and Grasping for Other Approaches

Whether or not passing laws and regulations is even the right approach for shaping the digital technology and the internet is a matter of debate. It's been suggested that altering underlying structures and creating new incentives for interoperability might have more of the desired impact than the top-down enforcement of rules. Interoperability simply means that different digital services can interact with each other, and that users have more control and ability to move between them than they currently do.

If the nature of online companies were more interoperable, the thinking goes, then big tech companies would not be so dominant, and consumers would have more choices and more control. Some people see this as a more desirable approach because it ostensibly returns the internet to its more essential, decentralized nature without top-down government intervention that could have unintended consequences.

> *I think we would benefit from taking a big step back from "pass a rule and enforce it" to think about different ways for government to intervene.*
>
> —CHRIS RILEY,
> GLOBAL INTERNET POLICY AND TECHNOLOGY RESEARCHER

> *There is a reason that compatibility tends to win out over the long run—it is the default state of the world—the sock company does not get to specify your shoes and the dairy does not get to dictate which cereal you pour milk over. But as technology markets have grown more concentrated and less competitive, what was once business-as-usual has become almost unthinkable…today's tech giants show every sign of establishing a permanent, dominant position over the internet.*
>
> —CORY DOCTOROW,
> AUTHOR AND JOURNALIST

PULLING IT TOGETHER

While there is certainly a place for adversarial, top-down government enforcement for technology, in many cases, government and technology are already trying to work together more productively and "move closer to each other." Whether through sandboxes or collaboration, bringing the public and private sectors closer together may help technology evolve in ways that are beneficial. How might we advance the cause to shape the world productively and move beyond a purely adversarial stance?

Something IS NOT RIGHT...

Proactive **POLICY** Reactive

It's hard to predict the future

BASICS
POLICY & DESIGN

HISTORIC
EMERGENT
HARMS

(NON-DIGITAL)

Present day EMERGENT HARMS

(DIGITAL)

~~INTERNAL~~
INTERVENTIONS

*Organizations create
their own policy*

EXTERNAL
INTERVENTIONS

*Government policy
in the digital sphere*

Designing
WITHIN
**POLICY
CONSTRAINTS**

Bringing
POLICY &
DESIGN

Closer Together

Bringing
**DESIGN
METHODS** TO POLICY
CREATION

Enterprise
Design
and
POLICY

WICKED
PROBLEMS
and Baby
Steps

9

Using Design to Create Better Policy

C ivic tech is a rich and growing field. Author and design leader Cyd Harrell defines it as "a loosely integrated movement that brings the strengths of the private-sector tech world (its people, methods, or actual technology) to public entities with the aim of making government more responsive, efficient, modern, and more just."[1] The field is vast and wide ranging, covering everything from turning PDFs into HTML to the redesign of public facing websites and large infrastructural database projects. The formation of policy discussed here is one aspect of that universe.

---

1. Cyd Harrell, *A Civic Technologist's Practice Guide* (Five Seven Five Books, 2020).

In the policy sphere, as of the early 2020s, designers typically worked on the *implementation* of policy rather than earlier on in the policy cycle (recall the policy process described in Chapter 2, "Policy and Design Basics"). For example, designers might work on a website that aimed to streamline applications for unemployment insurance, rather than on the decision to widen access to UI in the first place. However, using design methods in the *creation* of policy, rather than just its implementation, is a nascent space that is seeing new growth.

> *I'm really curious to see ways that design processes, research, and strategy can be used in other parts of the policy cycle— when you're setting policy intentions, forming policy, implementation, and evaluation. I think designers and design methods can be present in those other parts of the policy cycle. I have an urban planning background and I don't think you can plan behind a desk. Policymakers shouldn't hide behind a desk either. Some of these approaches that designers are really familiar with should be part of the policy cycle—to get out of the data—which is important—and form a more nuanced understanding of what's going on.*

> —ANGELICA QUICKSEY,
> DESIGN MANAGER AT NAVA

Using Design Methods in Policy Creation

It's a well-known truism in the software world that a big waterfall release, without user feedback allowing for pivots, is unlikely to result in a product that meets the real needs of people. Many spaces in the public sector are just beginning to adopt agile approaches in the development of software. Adopting such approaches in the creation of policy is perhaps even farther out. As Tom Loosemore of the UK Government Digital Service put it, "Why is policy still educated guesswork with a feedback loop measured in years?" However, new approaches are being articulated that attempt to bring iterative design upstream in the policy cycle.

Incorporating design tools and methods at various stages of the policy formation cycle is one straightforward way of doing so. Alberto Rodriguez Alvarez and Dana Chisnell, of the Beeck Center at Georgetown University, have created a "User-Centered Policy Design Map" to illustrate just that (see Figure 9.1). Their map suggests, for example, that ethnographic interviews can be used in agenda setting, and proof-of-concept testing used in policy formation. One could imagine journey maps and personas—standard tools in the design process—helping to inform policymakers of how their policies would impact people.

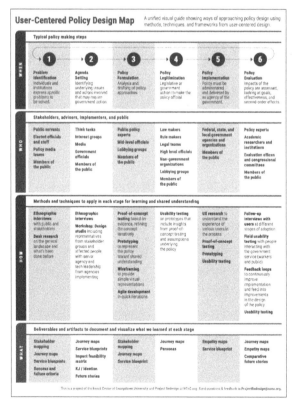

FIGURE 9.1 The User-Centered Policy Design Map connects steps in the policy creation process to well-known design methods.

While you shouldn't assume that all expert policymaking needs an overhaul, the top-down approach has some of the same pitfalls that big-release software processes do. Big policy changes can be just as high-risk as big software system cutovers. In particular, where policies are designed to benefit specific groups of people, but the designers aren't members of those communities, the same problems will crop up as when software design teams don't understand their users or have sufficient diversity. And when policy interventions are intended to influence individual behavior at scale, then a top-down, big-release process rests on a lot of assumptions and introduces a high level of risk.

—CYD HARRELL,
A CIVIC TECHNOLOGIST'S PRACTICE GUIDE

Iterative Releases Incorporating Feedback into Policy

In their shaping of "the future," both UX/product development and policy concern themselves with experiments and assessing impact as they put forth solutions to problems. Yet, feedback from prototypes is a less common practice in policy than it is in the tech world. Feedback from policy prototypes of the kind Alvarez and Chisnell recommend can then move *back upstream*, impacting how a policy is designed. As in software, the best results in policy materialize when visionary leaders articulate the desired outcomes or the "why," and allow smart implementation teams to solve creatively for the "how." But in the policy world, such an approach is often not the norm. Policies can include hundreds of pages of detailed specifications for how they should be implemented, which Tom Loosemore of the UK Government Digital Service says amount to a mountain of untested assumptions.

In her framework for "Delivery Driven Policy," from 2019, Jennifer Pahlka of Code for America cites the example of a failed policy implementation for SNAP benefits, otherwise known as *food stamps*. Because the policy as written included a restriction on when eligibility interviews for food stamps should be conducted, it left thousands of people, who could not make their interview appointment times, out of the benefit. If, instead, the policy had been implemented iteratively, policymakers might have realized that to be successful, flexibility for the interview times was necessary. Whether such iterative releases can stand up to the reality of being tested "in the real world" has yet to be seen.

In public policy evaluation, we do not usually have the luxury of a laboratory experiment. The whole process is much more complicated because real persons are involved… It is a fundamental truth that a causal result can never be estimated with 100% certainty. It is a probabilistic approach which attempts to simulate the conditions of an experiment so as to measure/estimate the impact of interest, with the least possible error.

—TAKIS VENETOKLIS,
SOCIAL POLICY RESEARCHER[2]

NOTE ➤ **The Principal-Agent Problem**

The "implementation gap"—where a well-intentioned policy can fail because the implementation details are wrong—is actually understood in some policy circles, and known as the "principal-agent problem." The stakeholder who delegates a task is known as the "principal," while the one executing the task is known as the "agent." When the principal cannot observe the efforts of the agent(s), the principal-agent problem arises, leading to overall failure of the policy to achieve its goals. Hence, bringing the principal and the agent—or policymaking and implementation— closer together could help avoid such problems.

2. Takis Venetoklis, "Public Policy Evaluation: Introduction to Quantitative Methodologies," *Research Reports from VATT Institute for Economic Research* (2002), https://econpapers .repec.org/paper/ferresrep/90.htm

"How It Looks" Can Change Policy

As discussed, iterative methods that provide feedback on policy implementation can move upstream and impact how policies are written. That idea has particular resonance when the public interacts with a physical artifact or any kind of interface: how the thing looks can impact how the policy is written and vice versa—how the policy is written can impact how the thing looks. Voting is a prime example, where the policies—around design of polling place signage or voting instructions, for example—can have deep impacts.

Take the design of absentee ballots. In the 2008 election for senator in Minnesota between Al Franken and Norm Coleman, a controversy over absentee ballots led to recounts and legal battles. Many of the ballots were disqualified because the envelope with the voter's identification and witness signature was not completed correctly. Effectively, citizens who had made the effort to receive and return a ballot did not have their votes counted.

After the election was decided, the state undertook a project with the Center for Civic Design and Whitney Quesenbery to revise the design of absentee ballots[3] (see Figures 9.2a and 9.2b). While the statutes about voting may have indicated in detail the absentee voting requirements, Quesenbery knew that starting with those words could lead to a poor design and voter experience. So, instead, her team started with the design of the absentee ballot, and then checked those designs against the words of the statute. In the end, the designs moved upstream and impacted how the policy was written.

3. Whitney Quesenbery, "Absentee Ballot Instructions in Minnesota," Center for Civic Design, (blog) https://civicdesign.org/showcase/absentee-ballot-instructions-in-minnesota/

INSTRUCTIONS FOR ABSENTEE VOTERS

Step 1. You must have a witness to vote by absentee ballot. Your witness may be anyone who is registered to vote in Minnesota including your spouse or another relative, ~~or they may be~~ a notary public or a person with the authority to administer oaths.

Step 2. Show your witness the unmarked ballot~~(s)~~.

Step 3. Mark your votes in private according to the instructions on the ballot(s). ~~Mark your ballot(s) in private. If you have a disability or are otherwise unable to mark the ballot(s), you may ask your witness to assist you.~~ Make sure you do not vote for more candidates than allowed for any office, since this will prevent your votes for that office from being counted. If you make an error ~~when marking your ballot, you may~~ request a new ballot ~~from the election official from whom you received your ballot~~. If you cannot request a new ballot, either completely erase any errors or draw a line through the name of the candidate(s) for whom you mistakenly voted and remark your ballot for your preferred candidate(s). Do not ~~put any identifying marks~~ write your name or an identification number anywhere on the ballot.

Instructions
How to vote by absentee ballot

Get ready
You will need:
- Ballot
- Tan ballot envelope
- Voter registration application
- White signature envelope

- Minnesota driver's license with your address or other authorized proof of where you live. *See the other side for options*
- Witness
  Someone registered to vote in Minnesota including your spouse or a relative, or any notary public, or a person with the authority to administer oaths

Important: You must submit the voter registration application with your ballot in the signature envelope for your vote to count.

❶ Fill out the voter registration application and sign it
- Show your witness your driver's license or other authorized proof of where you live. *See the other side for options.*

❷ Vote!
- Show your witness your ballot, then mark your votes in private.
- Follow the instructions on the ballot.
- Do not write your name or an ID number anywhere on the ballot.
- Do not vote for more candidates than allowed. *If you do, your votes for that office will not count.*
- *See the other side if you make a mistake on your ballot.*

❸ Seal your ballot in the tan ballot envelope
- Do not write on this envelope.

❹ Put the tan ballot envelope and the voter registration application into the top of the white signature envelope

❺ Complete the white signature envelope
- If there is no label, print your name and Minnesota address.
- Read and sign the oath.
  Your signature will be compared to the one on your absentee ballot application.
- Ask your witness to print their name and Minnesota address, indicate which proof you showed them, and sign their name.
  If your witness is an official, they must print their title, instead of their address. Notaries must affix their stamp.
- Seal the envelope. First the small flap, then the large flap.

❻ Return your ballot to the address on the signature envelope
Ballots may not be delivered directly to your polling place.
You have three options:
- Send it so it arrives by election day, using U.S. Mail or a package delivery service,
- Deliver it in person by 5:00 p.m. on the day before the election, or
- Ask someone to deliver it by 3:00 p.m. on election day.
  This person cannot deliver more than 3 ballots.

FIGURES 9.2A AND 9.2B The original design of the Minnesota absentee ballot instructions was based on the "letter of the law," rather than on design principles that would make the form easy to understand for readers. The redesign incorporated such principles, and it went on to influence policy.

Many states include the instructions for voting in the statute, where they cannot be changed easily…[this can] lock election officials into bad design requirements, such as the use of all-capitals or specific font sizes, [making] ballots harder to read and use…Even if a state does decide to improve the situation, changes are handled like a typical process of writing a new law, through reviews of "markup." With its focus on the words of the law, this process makes it almost impossible to check the legal requirements against a well-designed ballot or clearly written instructions.

—WHITNEY QUESENBERY,
DIRECTOR AND CO-FOUNDER OF THE CENTER FOR CIVIC DESIGN

PULLING IT TOGETHER

Policy centers on values, while design centers on users. Neither of these frames is better than the other, but they can learn from each other. Bringing methods of design into the policymaking process is a nascent space that is seeing new experimentation. Incorporating tools like interviews and journey mapping into policy creation, iterative releases, and allowing design principles to impact the way a policy is written are all things that are being attempted. As the policy and design spheres move closer together, each side has an opportunity to learn from the other, incorporating new methods up- and downstream in their respective processes.

Something IS NOT RIGHT...

Proactive ← POLICY → Reactive
It's hard to predict the future

BASICS
POLICY & DESIGN

HISTORIC EMERGENT HARMS
(NON-DIGITAL)

 Present day EMERGENT HARMS (DIGITAL)

INTERNAL INTERVENTIONS
Organizations create their own policy

EXTERNAL INTERVENTIONS
Government policy in the digital sphere

 Designing WITHIN POLICY CONSTRAINTS

Bringing POLICY & DESIGN Closer Together

Bringing DESIGN METHODS TO POLICY CREATION

 Enterprise Design and POLICY

WICKED PROBLEMS and Baby Steps

10

Enterprise Design and the Policy Space

I n the more highly regulated domains discussed in the previous chapter, we often saw what were referred to as "enterprises" and the accompanying uniqueness of enterprise design. Think of enterprise design as the internal tools that run organizations—from HR software, to document management tools, to workflow management software that dispatches repair people to jobs in the field. Enterprise design is a uniting aspect of both public sector and large private sector organizations. Why? They are both big and complex. This chapter is a description of the challenges of enterprise design, and a call to get excited about them, as meeting these challenges will determine how well the very infrastructure of societies functions.

Not Shiny New Tech

Key to enterprise design is that it is typically not consumer-facing, and is in many ways the antithesis of new tech companies like Spotify or Airbnb, which tend to attract young design talent (and where the harms of new tech tend to emerge). While enterprise design serves users just as consumer design does, enterprise users typically have no choice but to use the software mandated by their employers. As a result, much of the UX of enterprise software can get away with being scandalously bad.

This represents a juicy challenge for user-focused enterprise designers. Many of the sophisticated methods that designers take for granted in the consumer space are only just now beginning to seep into the darker corners of the enterprises that run our world. The back office systems behind communications, banking, healthcare, employment, supply chain, voting, and many other private and public domains are in desperate need of improvement. Methods like user research, agile development, and the incorporation of design are somewhat new in the enterprise space. Yet can the methods of consumer facing tech be mapped to enterprise one-to-one?

> *Most people don't choose enterprise—they just end up there, and if they like it, they stay.*
>
> —YICHEN HE,
> ENTERPRISE UX DESIGNER

Challenges to Developing an Enterprise Design Playbook

In *The Lean Startup*, author Eric Ries described the methods that tech startups can use to be successful—things like build-measure-learn, promoting small experiments, and pivoting—in other words, the tenets of agile development. In *The Startup Way*, Ries attempted to take lessons from his previous book and apply them to other business types, like the more established ones discussed here. When the rubber meets the road on these strictures, however, startup methods don't map quite perfectly to larger enterprises. As design leader Cyd Harrell describes it in her book, *A Civic Technologist's Practice Guide*, one reason is that the concept of "customers" is not quite the same in the public sector as it is in the private sector.

> *Implementing something like Agile with success relies on answering questions about what a product is for, how customers value it, and how the company measures success. Government agencies thinking of their work as policy don't typically need to address these product questions with the same urgency, and NGOs don't view themselves as competing for customers. Without those underlying answers, a method that depends on the entire team being able to collectively answer the question "What should we focus on to advance our core goal?" every two weeks—with the potential of being able to shift that goal on the table, no less—is going to be much harder.*
>
> —CYD HARRELL,
> *A CIVIC TECHNOLOGIST'S PRACTICE GUIDE*

Yichen He is a designer who has made a career in enterprise spaces, and who has written about what she sees as the exciting challenges of a career in Enterprise UX Design.[1] She notes that another of the key reasons that Enterprise UX takes a back seat to consumer UX is the NDA (non-disclosure agreement)—the fact that enterprise design work that is exemplary or educational cannot be freely talked about since it is internal to organizations and subject to restrictions. Thus, creating a playbook for Enterprise UX will take some creativity in order to generalize to the point of making the lessons useful.

---

1. Yichen He, "Designing for Enterprise vs. Designing for Consumers," *UX Collective* (blog), December 10, 2020, https://uxdesign.cc/designing-for-enterprise-vs-designing-for-consumers-36a16f2281c2

Critical Gaps in Enterprise Design

The previous section isn't meant to suggest that enterprise spaces can't benefit from improvement—in fact, they are in desperate need of it. But mapping an old playbook onto this space is unlikely to work. Instead, a new playbook is needed. The following section is a noncomprehensive list of some of the critical gaps that would need to be addressed in a new playbook. Many of these gaps challenge notions around user-centricity and the need to implement it differently in enterprise spaces.

Legacy Systems

One thing that large organizations—public and private—have in common is that they have generally been around for a lot longer than newer startups or tech companies. Starting a new, modern company with new, modern tools is bound to result in an organized, efficiently functioning system. But trying to retrofit old systems into new modern tools? That's many orders of magnitude harder. Migrating from old, legacy systems to new ones is painful, yet critical work, which can take years and often does not immediately touch users. Thus, there are a few clear ways to "learn" from users and pivot based on learnings.

That said, sometimes migrating from old systems to new is unnecessary and counterproductive. Take the example of the 60-year-old COBOL programming language, which runs many state unemployment systems. The software works fine, but requires skilled programmers to upkeep the code (as code does). Because the software is old, it has been heavily disinvested, which caused the sites to cave when users flooded unemployment systems in the Covid-19 pandemic. While many in the programming community blamed the COBOL language, in reality the culprit was disinvestment in old systems that worked just fine.

In this sense, COBOL and its scapegoating show us an important aspect of high tech that few in Silicon Valley, or in government, seem to understand. Older systems have value, and constantly building new technological systems for short-term profit at the expense of existing infrastructure is not progress. In fact, it is among the most regressive paths a society can take.

—MAR HICKS,
"BUILT TO LAST"[2]

How might we create space for smart, evidence-informed infrastructural work outside of the build-measure-learn formulation of Agile, and which does not simply innovate for innovation's sake?

Users Have No Choice

As mentioned previously, users in enterprises typically have no choice but to use the tools that their employers mandate. Thus, metrics like engagement and adoption (which consumer-facing tech uses to track its success) simply do not apply. Yet designing for users is unequivocally important, even in the enterprise space, just as it is in the consumer space. This challenge is even more pronounced in the public sector, which, on top of often catering to internal employees, also does not have a profit motive and the obvious measurements that naturally come along with it.

How might we reimagine metrics that measure the value of user-centricity—whether that's employee retention, efficiency, improved insights, or other metrics—when employees have no choice but to use the tool in question? Can we clearly tie the user experience of employees to metrics that their employers care about?

2. Mar Hicks, "Built to Last," *Logic Magazine*, Issue 11, August 31, 2020, https://logicmag.io/care/built-to-last/

Build vs. Buy

In large enterprises, the build versus buy question is a critical one that often arises. Yet whether to build custom software or buy it off the shelf and modify it is one question that designers and technologists in consumer-facing tech (which is pretty much all "build") are ill-equipped to answer. What's more, customizing off-the-shelf software to serve the specific needs of a user group is something that traditional design tends not to address. Whether a CRM or EHR (Electronic Health Record) software, modifying these tools from their out-of-the-box state is a complex, and often many years-long, process.

How might we equip designers and engineers for the critical decision-making and customization surrounding off-the-shelf software?

Solutions in Search of Problems

In Chapter 4, "Unconstrained Spaces and the Emergence of Harm," we explored the "search for use cases" in new tech—the idea that some new tech is developed, and designers go out trying to figure out how it fits into the world. This idea runs counter to the often repeated notion in the design world of "understanding a problem first, and only then developing a solution." Enterprise spaces are similarly rife with solutions in search of problems, rather than the other way around. Whether it's one of the off-the-shelf tools mentioned previously, or the classic example of bringing email into the workplace, designers are often tasked with figuring out how to fit some piece of new technology into a workforce, rather than starting with understanding their problems.

How might we reimagine the concept of "problem-solution" for the reality of spaces where tools are mandated?

Policy Constraints

It perhaps does not need to be repeated at this point, but larger enterprises are constrained by policy in ways that startups aren't. The medical, finance, and many other societal domains must deal with legal strictures in their areas. This can slow down release times, and runs counter to the "fail fast" dogma of new technology. And, as explored in Chapter 7, "Design in Policy-Constrained Domains," it can introduce friction into the user experience that does not exist in unregulated areas.

How might we reimagine release cycles that build in policy concerns?

Facilitation: A Key Enterprise Skill Gap

While this book has to do with digital design and software, the grease between the wheels of the machine is people. And that may be even more true in enterprise spaces with their overlapping pieces of infrastructure and stakeholder responsibilities. Because of this, facilitation is one of the key missing gaps for designers, or anyone, working in large organizations. Let's take an example to illustrate.

Imagine that there are two internal work processes—the first creates "golden source" data that lives on an outdated database. It includes a large amount of complicated workflow processes around validating and adding the data. The second process adds a few important data points to that golden source, but they are related to completely different work processes, which relate to different people and have nothing to do with the first process. A new, more modern system is desired for the second process to add its data points more easily. But how to do this? Should process one, with all of its complexities, be moved wholesale over to this new system? Or should it stay intact, and those who create the data have new responsibilities for entering it into two places? (Data extraction processes are not an option here because the new and old systems are too different.)

Exploring different ideas, getting the stakeholders to empathize with one another's needs and pain points, considering big picture priorities of the institution, and coming to a conclusion together on the path forward is the only way that this project will be successful. A solution brought down from "on high" could upset everyone and sink the undertaking. Yet designers often lack the skills to plan out an engagement that takes stakeholders on a decision-making and prioritization journey of this kind. There are enormous needs for facilitation of just this nature across enterprise spaces, and the design field would do well to teach and mentor sophisticated facilitation skills.

> *We have no choice. We have to stay at the table. There is no alternative... I now understand that collaboration is the only way to solve problems. I do it now in everything I do, including running my business and dealing with my suppliers, employees and customers.*
>
> —UNNAMED BUSINESSMAN AND ELECTED OFFICIAL QUOTED IN ACADEMIC PAPER, "COLLABORATIVE POLICYMAKING: GOVERNANCE THROUGH DIALOGUE," BY JUDITH E. INNES AND DAVID E. BOOHER[3]

On Bigness and Complexity

Yet another gap in enterprise design is the need to grapple with concepts of bigness and complexity. The way our systems interact in large organizations, both public and private, includes overlapping functions and priorities that make them difficult to grasp in their totality, and thus predict how they will work.

---

3. Judith E. Innes and David E. Booher, "Collaborative Policymaking: Governance Through Dialogue," in *Deliberative Policy Analysis*, ed. Maarten A. Hajer and Hendrik Wagenaar (Cambridge University Press, 2003), www.csus.edu/indiv/s/shulockn/executive%20 fellows%20pdf%20readings/innes%20and%20booher%20collaborative%20 policymaking.pdf

In his book, *Overcomplicated: Technology at the Limits of Comprehension*, Samuel Arbesman uses the analogy of water buoys to explain complex systems. Buoys floating in water, connected to each other by a rope, will be impacted by the wake of a boat sailing by. But the fact that the buoys are connected to each other causes unexpected feedback, and if the boat had sailed by at a slightly different angle, it would have had a totally different impact. Then imagine the buoys thrown onto a dock. The way they are arranged may be intricate, but it is ultimately static and could be described in a coherent fashion. The buoys on the dock are complicated, while the ones in the water are complex.

The systems that run large enterprises are similarly complex. Take again the concept of data. A large organization might want to organize data at the org-wide enterprise level. But within this organization are many smaller groups that have their own data needs and taxonomies, and those might not all fit together neatly at a higher level. The organization itself may have multiple geographic locations. Add on the fact that the organization is constantly collecting new data with new attributes, and the system becomes complex. Changing one part of the process, or the software that runs it, could have unexpected implications up- or downstream.

> *When an outcome is unexpected, it means that we don't have the level of understanding necessary to see how it occurred. If it's a bug in a video game, this can be delightful or even entertaining. But when we encounter unexpected situations in the complex systems that allow our society to function—the infrastructure that provides our power and water, or the software that allows financial transactions to occur, or the program that prevents planes from colliding midair—it's not entertaining at all. Lack of understanding becomes a matter of life and death.*
>
> —SAMUEL ARBESMAN,
> OVERCOMPLICATED: TECHNOLOGY AT THE LIMITS OF COMPREHENSION

Systems thinking and systems design may increasingly look to fill gaps in these spaces. Designing by considering elements outside of software could help designers grapple with complexity and unforeseen consequences—systems thinking scholar and author Donella Meadows has urged a focus on structures (institutions), relationships (stakeholders and power dynamics), and paradigms (culture and mindsets).[4] Still, much of systems design is framed with the "consumer" or "user" lens, rather than an enterprise one. It, too, may need to be rethought to meet enterprise challenges.

> *Designers are entrusted with increasingly complex and impactful challenges. However, the current system of design education does not always prepare students for these challenges.*
>
> —MICHAEL W. MEYER AND DON NORMAN,
> CHANGING DESIGN EDUCATION FOR THE 21ST CENTURY

4. Donella Meadows, "Leverage Points: Places to Intervene in a System," *The Sustainability Institute* (1999), https://donellameadows.org/archives/leverage-points-places-to-intervene-in-a-system/

PULLING IT TOGETHER

The public sector and large organizations are big and complex, and they use enterprise software to run their systems. This is an area that has been comparatively overlooked by the design community, yet how well it functions is critical to how well our world's infrastructure operates. Looking at some of the "gaps" in enterprise design—including the fact that internal users have no choice but to adopt the systems in question—could yield a playbook for designing in these enterprise, policy-constrained spaces. All of this represents an exciting opportunity for idealistic designers seeking a challenge.

Something IS NOT RIGHT...

Proactive **POLICY** Reactive
It's hard to predict the future

BASICS POLICY & DESIGN

HISTORIC EMERGENT HARMS
(NON-DIGITAL)

Present day EMERGENT HARMS **(DIGITAL)**

INTERVENTIONS
Organizations create their own policy

EXTERNAL
INTERVENTIONS
Government policy in the digital sphere

Designing WITHIN **POLICY CONSTRAINTS**

Bringing POLICY & DESIGN
Closer Together

Bringing **DESIGN METHODS** TO POLICY CREATION

Enterprise Design AND POLICY

WICKED PROBLEMS and Baby Steps

Wicked Problems and Baby Steps

Humans are not good at predicting what the impacts of our technologies will be. This is why VCs back bets in hundreds of tech "experiments," in the hopes that even just one will have uptake. We also generally have a hard time predicting which harms will emerge from things that *do* end up being used. And, once harms emerge, we have competing interests of capitalism and social values to contend with when addressing them. Just like enterprise software, solving for problems of emerging technology and addressing them with policy is a complex space.

One might even go so far as to characterize the overarching challenges of "solving" for harms of new technology as a "wicked problem." Major social problems (which policy attempts to address), such as housing the unhoused, are often characterized as "wicked" because they share a few key characteristics: the involvement of many different stakeholders with different or competing priorities, incomplete knowledge, and their interconnected nature. These characteristics make them hard to fix.

Some thinkers have suggested that the entire undertaking of solving wicked problems is futile. In his tongue-in-cheek book, *Systemantics: How Systems Work and Especially How They Fail,* John Gall notes that trying to solve some problem with a new system creates new problems, and that the amount of "mess" in the world never really lessens, instead just shifting to different places.

> *When a system is set up to accomplish some goal, a new entity has come into being—the system itself. No matter what the "goal" of the system, it immediately begins to exhibit system behavior; that is, to act according to the general laws that govern the operation of all systems. Now the system itself has to be dealt with. Whereas before, there was only the problem—such as warfare between nations, or garbage collection—there is now an additional universe of problems associated with the functioning or merely the presence of the new system.*

> —JOHN GALL,
> *SYSTEMANTICS*

For this reason, in the words of sustainable design professor Robert Knapp, a better approach to wicked problems is "intervention," rather than "solution."[1] This recognizes that big problems are simply mitigated and set on a more positive overall trajectory, rather than solved outright. Small, cautious steps that appear directionally more correct may be the best that we can hope for—especially when it comes to policymaking.

1. Robert Knapp, "Wholesome Design for Wicked Problems," *Public Sphere Project* (blog), www.publicsphereproject.org/content/wholesome-design-wicked-problems

Making policy is at best a very rough process. Neither social scientists, nor politicians, nor public administrators yet know enough about the social world to avoid repeated error in predicting the consequences of policy moves. A wise policymaker consequently expects that [their] policies will achieve only part of what [they] hope and at the same time will produce unanticipated consequences [they] would have preferred to avoid. If [they] proceed through a succession of incremental changes, [they] avoid serious lasting mistakes.

—CHARLES E. LINDBLOM,
THE SCIENCE OF MUDDLING THROUGH

On the "these problems are hard to solve" note, many times while writing this book, I would remind myself and my editor and publisher that this was not intended to be a "how-to" book. Well, perhaps it was 20% "how-to do" and 80% "how-to think." Essentially, my feeling has always been that establishing a mental model *is* the how-to because the intersection of policy and design is such a dense space.

But everyone loves productive next steps. So I'll end on a summary of some of the exhortations, geared toward both technologists and policymakers, that popped up throughout the book. There is no one simple answer to fixing this space, but by poking at the problem with some of these methods, perhaps we'll move things in a good direction.

- Consider the distinction between "pain points" and "harms"—designers look for the former, but usually not the latter. Might we widen the lens?

- Try to prevent harms of bias and discrimination before they emerge by proactively targeting designs to those most likely to be harmed and other methods described in the book—but understand that that's not always possible.

- While we're bad at predicting what will happen, it's a pretty safe bet that abuse will be a thing, and whatever is bad will be worse for some people than others.

- Keep a cautious eye out for harms and notice when they do emerge. When that happens, raise a flag, bond with other employees, or appeal to your "top-down buddy"—in other words, make your reactive responses as proactive as possible.

- Write guidelines and best practices. These can harden into policies down the line.

- It's always a good time to plant seeds for future mental models. Write, talk, start a group of interest around a particular topic, and build shared understanding about the future.

- Stay abreast of what policy and design are up to. Understand how each works. Build bridges between the two.

- For policymakers, can you connect with those on the frontlines designing the future?

- For designers or technologists, develop subject matter expertise in your domain. Get curious about how policy intersects with it. Can you develop a point of view on how policy *should* impact it and move "upstream" to influence that?

- Lean into the tough, messy spaces that underpin our society. Do you have anything to add to a desperately needed enterprise design playbook? Democracy, and society's critical infrastructure, need you.

- Above all, collaborate. Work your facilitation skills. Get people in a room talking, particularly ones who don't often interact, and stay at the table.

Index

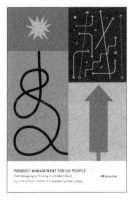

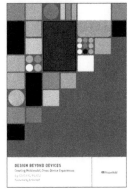

Acknowledgments

I am thankful to the many people who have written about the topics covered in this book, or taken the time to speak with me about them. I also want to thank those people behind the scenes, whose support and ideas helped me throughout the years-long process of writing this book.

For making the book significantly better with their insightful comments and feedback: Conor Friedersdorf, Angelica Quicksey, Samit Sura, and Chris Riley.

For believing in me and encouraging me: Jess Dale, Matt Holzman, Maria Massei-Rosato, and Dominique Lee.

For advice on book writing: Saul Austerlitz, Jessica Koosed-Etting, and Laura Klein.

Collaborators and work community: Aaron Gitlin, Kate Wulfson, Arielle Wiltz, Theo Linnemann, Jim Chan, Rachel Robbins, Natalie Blair, Justin Poston, Emily Parcell, Ginger Reinauer, Eddie Tejeda, and Lisa Baskett.

Family and friends: Dyanne, Ryan, Shira, Tali, Shana, Eyal, Noah, Eve, Ellen, Rory, Sharmilli, Taylor, Charlotte, Adi, Aucher, Sasha, Alex G., Nancy, Suzy, Tony, Jason, Gary, Michele, Michael, Kat, Aaron, Anita, Ariela, Amy, Molly, Ari, Orly, Gabi, Sammy, and most of all, my parents, Susan and Isaac.

Thank you to Lou Rosenfeld for reading my articles on privacy and believing I might have a book in me, all those years back. Thanks to MJ Broadbent, whose brilliant illustrations and exceptional client service were the cherry on top of writing this book. And a special thanks to the other MJ, Marta Justak, for her sharp editorial eye and for striking the perfect balance between taskmaster and friend. I deeply appreciate her patience, compassion, deadlines, and interest in my personal trials and tribulations.

About the Author

ALEX SCHMIDT has pursued interests in public service and design through different avenues over her career. As an award-winning reporter and producer for NPR and others, she covered arts, business, technology, and urban development. Alex has published work in *The New Yorker* and *The Los Angeles Times*, among other outlets. Her writing about UX, privacy, and other design topics has appeared in *A List Apart* and *The Columbia Journalism Review.*

As a researcher, strategist, and UX designer, Alex has worked both for agencies and in the public sector. Her greatest interest lies in the wicked problems inherent in enterprise design and the mysterious ways of large systems. These are all areas she has delved into as a product strategist for The Federal Reserve Bank of New York.

CPSIA information can be obtained
at www.ICGtesting.com
Printed in the USA
JSHW020229021022
31225JS00001B/1

9 781933 820156